Opal Sunset

ALSO BY CLIVE JAMES

CLIVE JAMES

Opal Sunset

SELECTED POEMS 1958–2008

PICADOR

Essex County Council Libraries

First published 2008 by W. W. Norton & Company, Inc.

First published in Great Britain 2009 by Picador
an imprint of Pan Macmillan Ltd
Pan Macmillan, 20 New Wharf Road, London N1 9RR
Basingstoke and Oxford
Associated companies throughout the world
www.panmacmillan.com

ISBN 978-0-330-46817-6

Copyright © Clive James 2008

1 3 5 7 9 8 6 4 2

A CIP catalogue record for this book is available from
the British Library.

Printed in the UK by CPI Mackays, Chatham ME5 8TD

Visit **www.picador.com** to read more about all our books
and to buy them. You will also find features, author interviews and
news of any author events, and you can sign up for e-newsletters
so that you're always first to hear about our new releases.

To Robert Weil

Contents

A Note on the Text

The poems in this selection are drawn from two main reservoirs of work. In the contents list, all the poems up to and including 'The Great Wrasse' (a word which the people of Australia's Great Barrier Reef pronounce with two syllables, to rhyme with sassy) are selected from *The Book of My Enemy: Collected Verse 1958–2003*, a much larger volume which is still in print in Britain and Australia. The last poem in the contents list, 'As I See You', also appears in that book, leading the section marked 'Earlier Verse' in its role as the first poem of mine that ever saw the light of day: I have employed it as a closing number here because of the neatness with which it signifies that I somehow, at the age of eighteen, started off with my sense of impending doom already intact. Apart from all those poems, no poem on the list from 'Status Quo Vadis' (whose title is a howler I stole from the movie *Strictly Ballroom*) to 'The Nymph Calypso' has yet appeared in volume form anywhere, although all of them first appeared in any one of several newspapers and magazines whether in Britain, Australia or the United States.

The book thus breaks roughly into halves, with the selected work of my first forty-five years as a poet forming the first half, and the selected work of the next five forming the second; but I hope the apparent disproportion doesn't mean that I have been less rigorous about choosing the later poems. What has happened to me in recent

Footnote: Since the American edition of this book was published in 2008, some of the later poems have appeared in my 2009 Picador collection *Angels Over Elsinore*.

years will be familiar to anybody who does this sort of thing for a living: I hit a productive streak. I was just lucky enough to hit it late, when a lot of things I had always wanted to say were at last ready to be written down. It isn't so much that you finally get good enough to say it. It's that it finally agrees to be said.

Acknowledgements

My thanks are due to the editors of *The New Yorker*, the *New York Times*, *Poetry* (Chicago), the *Australian*, the *Australian Book Review*, the *Australian's Review of Books*, the *Australian Literary Review*, the *Monthly*, *Meanjin*, *Encounter*, the *Listener*, the *London Review of Books*, the *New Review*, the *New Statesman*, the *Liberal*, the *Spectator*, the *Guardian* and the *Times Literary Supplement*, in which many of the poems from which these were selected first appeared. Even when I failed to gain acceptance, I always got consideration; and since nobody wants to be published by the kind of editor who prints everything, I have always tried not to gripe when one of them bounces my latest effort. Often enough, they are right, and, more than often enough, they actually print one of my poems, an event that has never lost its thrill for me in half a century. Like any old hand I like to think myself cool, but I have never quite managed to take it for granted when I see my poem on the page. They say that when he landed after his first trip through the sound barrier, even Chuck Yeager cracked a smile.

Speaking of editors, my special thanks should go to Alan Jenkins, Karl Miller, Anthony Thwaite, Claire Tomalin, John Gross, Tina Brown, Alice Quinn, Christian Wiman, Mary-Kay Wilmers, Ben Ramm, Mark Amory and the late Ian Hamilton, all of whom, at various times, played uncomplaining host to the kind of guest who not only moves in, but spreads himself out. I should also, on a point of national pride, acknowledge the generosity of Shelley Gare, Les Murray, Peter Porter, Peter Rose, Sally Warhaft, Luke Slattery, Donata Carrazza, Peter Craven, Judith Beveridge and Stephen Romei, for their gratifying conviction that some of my work in verse should be brought home to Australia, the land that continues to inspire it all, even when I have been so long away. I should say at this point, however, that I am nowadays very often shuttling between my two homelands, and that several poems in this book were composed at high altitude. The Atlantic run, also, has become a steadily more favourable mobile *atelier* for verse, especially when the aircraft is surfing in the jet-stream: somehow the extra speed gets into one's scansion.

I should also thank my book editors in London, Tom Maschler, Peter Straus and Andrew Kidd, for their generosity in countenancing the sort of publishing venture that joins the bottom line to the far horizon. Finally, my thanks to Robert Weil in New York, who took a chance on my prose book *Cultural Amnesia*, and now compounds the audacity by introducing an almost unknown foreign poet to an American audience. Ideally, of course, the poet doesn't have to be known. The book of poems only has to be good. But someone has to publish it first.

Introduction

During fifty years of writing verse, I have never wavered from the conviction that the self-contained poem is the thing that matters. I have written longer poems, but I always thought that they should not, in their constituent episodes, wander too far from the appreciable unity of the stand-alone poem which could be committed to memory and recited aloud by anyone who wanted to. A poem should make you want to say it even if you don't understand it: that, indeed, is how you recognize it to be worth the effort of trying to understand.

Unfortunately, as I argued in my book of critical prose *Cultural Amnesia*, there is a penalty to be paid by any field of creative endeavour that becomes a successful commodity. Ceasing to be pursued for its own sake, poetry becomes a career move, and proves its academic prestige by deliberately putting itself out of reach of common appreciation. In the later part of the twentieth century the idea built up that a poet might go a long way towards writing poems that could not be spoken aloud at all even in the merest moments of their language, and that this development might even be considered an advance in the art form. There would be no local coherence, even in a single line. The poet would be appreciated through a 'body of work'. As a consequence, the separable poems no longer needed to be the thing that counted most in the total achievement of a professional poet with a reputation. I have never trusted that idea, partly because, having been blessed, or cursed, with the knack of earning my bread in show business, I was seldom regarded as a proper professional poet, and for a long while had no poetic reputation to speak of, except perhaps as a kind of court jester who was occasionally allowed to perch in a window niche and sing a lament over the ruins of the night's revelry.

In the course of time most of my earlier critics – the ones who were always keen to remind the world that I was only an entertainer – either died off or went silent, and I was allowed to have some kind of reputation anyway. But I still clung to the idea that the poem came first and the poet's name came second. I didn't think that a poet's name should be remarked unless the poems were remarkable. That priority of valuation first got into my head when I was a student at Sydney University in the late 1950s. Modern poetry was not a subject on the course, and therefore I read it with redoubled passion. Though I paid proper attention to the longer works of Ezra Pound and T. S. Eliot, even to the extent of memorising what struck me as the best bits, it was the shorter poems of W. H. Auden and Louis MacNeice that got me in. When I first read Auden's 'September 1939' I almost passed out from admiration, and MacNeice's 'Sunlight on the Garden' I can still recite from memory, having learned it on the first day I saw it. The impact of these brief pieces was like a vision of love, and still is: even now, there are individual lyric poems, sometimes by people I have never previously heard of, that knock me sideways. In all my life, that is still the effect that I most hope to have myself, and each of the eighty-two poems in this book has been chosen in the hope that it might do that to someone who has never heard my name.

If a poet makes a name, it should evoke a particular tone of voice. One of my particular early favourites was E. E. Cummings, always spelt e. e. cummings in those days, both at his own insistence and out of a widely shared admission that he had earned the right to his personal orthography because he had done so much to light up the visual element of the poem on the page. I didn't trust this latter claim for a minute. I adored his rhythmic swing and sexy humour, but his tricks of typography and layout seemed to me as mechanical as a rusting tractor, and just as obsolete. By now, the world-wide deployment of poetry that looks like shrapnel has wearied us of such effects, but the sad truth is that their chief inventors – Apollinaire got there before Cummings – wore them out instantly, because there was never any way you could say them. Considering that there was no way I could *not* say some of Cummings's lyrics and satires, the putative inventiveness of his typographical graffiti looked like what it was: the compensatory razzmatazz of a failed painter.

But there was nothing failed about those Cummings poems that demanded to be spoken. Committing a couple of his love lyrics to memory, I recited them unprompted to potential girlfriends. Most of these remained potential, but they were impressed, as they ought to have been. Though he was much more of a natural fascist than I then realised, Cummings was magic when he was in love, and when being funny he was more magical still. 'I sing of Olaf glad and big' became my party piece. The urge to write party pieces of my own was born at about that time, and it has never left me, probably because I'm still trying to get better at it.

Having exiled myself to London in the early 1960s, I was short of outlets. The literary editor of the student newspaper in Sydney had regularly accepted my poems because I was the literary editor. In London I held no such post and had to get used to the idea of writing poems that were not published. Since I went on writing them anyway, the evidence accumulated that I was serious, in my motivation if not in my achievement. I had new examples now of what seriousness looked like. It wasn't always solemn. Kingsley Amis (whose reputation as a novelist continues even now to mask his stature as a poet) was often outright funny, and Philip Larkin, my new top favourite, had such a range of tones that he could give sheer despair its enchanting moments. Larkin, indeed, was the exemplar of the poet whose creations were articulate in every part. But he exemplified the poet only in that he gave everything he had to each poem, including the love and energy that might have been devoted to a less restricted private life. He was dignified about his role, but he didn't expect it to be taken at face value without the poems to sustain it.

Thus was a lasting lesson made apprehensible to anyone with ears to hear. It was the poems that counted. Larkin was the author of poems like 'Lines on a Young Lady's Photograph Album' and 'The Whitsun Weddings'. They were compulsorily sayable, and it was his profusion of sayable poems that made him a poet. As I forged on with my own efforts, the standard that I was falling below got higher and higher. At Cambridge I decided that Thom Gunn's stronger poems came early on, and that the same applied to Ted Hughes. The same already applied to Robert Lowell, although the full emptiness of his careerist productivity still lay in the future. I liked those Marianne Moore poems that highlighted her phrase-making rather than her syllabic intricacy. When Robert Graves recommended Norman Cameron, I was embarrassed to find that I preferred the obscure Cameron to his luminous sponsor, because there were so few unarguably successful poems among Graves's many, and so many among Cameron's few. Solemnly I re-evaluated Dylan Thomas, having long ago realised that 'Fern Hill' was largely a put-up job, along with almost everything he had ever written longer than a page, but having finally realised that 'In My Craft or Sullen Art' was a little masterpiece that justified a lifetime of midnight flits and borrowed money. Both at Cambridge and later on in Fleet Street, I would recite that poem in the pub and defy my helpless interlocutors to identify the poet. The mention of the raging moon usually gave it away.

In the work of all these poets and many others, the distinction became ever clearer between poems that were written out of inspiration and those – usually the overwhelming bulk – that were written to keep up the reputation. Part of Sylvia Plath's tragedy was that her last poems were the most her, as it were; the brilliantly observed and imagined poem about her cut thumb outclassed so much of her previous work that had been sweated on ('working on a book of poems' was always a deadly phrase) to put her young name on the map. Among other Americans, it was most conspicuously Richard Wilbur that I revered for his high number of perfectly achieved things, but it was because I revered the things, not the public figure: he was dedicated and scholarly and clearly determined to last a long time, but what made him an exemplar was that he had written poems like 'A Baroque Wall-Fountain in the Villa Sciarra' and might write more. Many years later – too late to catch him while he was alive – I discovered Anthony Hecht through one poem in an old anthology. It was called 'Japan' and I thought it was perfect. I still do.

And so it went on for decade after decade of accumulating inspirations to fuel my own impulse. Sometimes it was a matter of rediscovering someone unfairly belittled early on. Edna St Vincent Millay's best love sonnets were really a lot better than I had at first thought. Elinor Wylie, whose high-flown pretensions had long been laughed at when she was remembered at all, had written at least one poem ('Wild Peaches') so strongly phrased that it committed itself to my memory without permission. The same applied to Charlotte Mew, to Keith Douglas, to Mervyn Peake: each had at least one poem with its own life. (Mervyn Peake's is about Belsen, and ought to be as famous as Paul Celan's 'Todesfuge'.) In Australia, my ever-beckoning homeland, there was James McAuley. Why had I never realised that his quietly desperate lyric 'Because', with its mesmerising phonetic punch, put him up there with the very best of Kenneth Slessor and A. D. Hope?

In any language that I can read – there were several of them as the years went by – I was always looking for the poetic phrases that, as Eliot said, communicated before they were understood, and I always found that they had been looking for me. That feeling of being chosen by the language, I think, is a common property of all readers and writers of poetry: it's the invasion of a body snatcher. But the takeover makes you more individual, not less. In Cambridge I had been published frequently in the university magazines, of which I was not always the literary editor; and later on, in Fleet Street, I got poems into the serious periodicals even while I was functioning as a TV critic and literary journalist. Then as now, I made a point of sending nothing out that I did not think sprang from a solid idea, and not just from the urge to gain recognition for an additional string to my bow. When I moved full-time into television I went on sending out any poem that I thought had a right to independent life. Finally I sent out a poem called 'The Book of My Enemy Has Been Remaindered', and even my most determined critics began to admit that I might have a voice. In the long run, that's the only moment of validation that matters. One absorbs many an influence, but only in the cause of sounding more like oneself. To the extent that I can tell, I never copied anyone, and am still careful not to do so, except through the occasional admiring allusion. I don't believe that poetry can fall into styles, periods or even into genres, because I don't believe in poetry, as such. I believe in poems, which come one at a time, and out of nowhere, and prove themselves to be something substantial only by their impact, like meteorites.

Streaking in through your eye to lodge deep in your head, the strong line is always the first sign of a poem's life. An arresting poem might have only a few of them, or even only one. (Very few admirers of William Empson's mighty line 'And now she cleans her teeth into the lake' can recite the rest of the poem, but they all know that that line is by Empson, and know that a glittering handful of such lines *are* Empson.) But if it has no strong lines at all, then it doesn't start. There can be such a thing as a counterfeit poem by the original author: an accomplished poem written in the poet's own manner, recognizable at every point as a poem by him yet with nothing driving it except the habitual urge to add yet another poem to his store. He is likely to be especially submissive to that urge in later life. The results, alas, are often flat. They contribute to what the academics who draw a salary from studying him would like to call his body of work, or his total achievement, or his poetry. But as Robert Frost tried to warn them in advance, if they are not talking about the poet's poems, they are usually talking about nothing. A poet courts such extended flatness when he starts to believe in his own career: an acreage of the self-similar, the architecture of a car-park.

Condemned by circumstance, for most of my life, to not having a career as a poet, I have sometimes fretted from the neglect, but always enjoyed the lack of responsibility. It could also be that I have enjoyed a crucial freedom. I have never been a prisoner of anything except the strangely inescapable duty to realise the idea when it comes. There are occasions when the idea itself is not real and never can be, and one works long and hard on something that refuses to come alive. Frequently the labour amounts to such an investment that one is reluctant to admit having given birth to a dud. I hope I have left most of those occasions out. Everything here, in its author's opinion at least, is the result of the genuine bolt from the blue. Randall Jarrell, a classic case of the industrious modern poet who wrote only a few real poems among the many in his own manner, said truly that a poet must wait to be struck by lightning. All poets believe it but few wait.

The lightning strike is as unmistakable as it was for Lee Trevino on the golf course. But it comes so seldom, and hits so hard, that you can't blame a literary operator for wanting to insure against its damnable infrequency. That, sadly, is the true story of modern formless poetry in general. Its aim is to insure against the occasional nature of inspiration by engaging in the continuous production of a kind of verbal plasma that can be cut off into marketable lengths. I only wish I could do it: life would be a lot easier. But I can't shake the belief that the self-contained poem is the thing that matters.

Nearing old age now, I have put in enough unpaid time at this activity to prove that the title of poet is one I might claim, if it is permissible to do other things and still claim it. My volume of collected verse, *The Book of My Enemy*, which came out in 2003, was greeted by the next generation of British and Australian critics in terms which must have set the previous generation spinning in their graves. They had so often found me guilty of sounding as if I were having too much fun, and now here were this new bunch suggesting that I just might be – with due allowance for the poisonously long half-life of television celebrity – some kind of poet after all.

But none of that will matter unless at least some of the pieces of writing in this much smaller book strike the reader as being poems. I have called it *Opal Sunset* because in my home city the sun goes down through a pink and azure sky, and because my beginnings are still with me. Indeed I have ended the book with the first poem I ever had published, fifty years ago. A student friend of mine learned it and quoted it back to me. I don't think he was just hitting me for a cigarette, although I staked him to a whole pack as a reward. In a culture growing weak from forgetfulness, to be memorable should be the aim. Remembering is a sign of recognition. Whether from the poet or the reader, recognition of the poetic moment is unequivocal: suddenly nothing else counts, and for as long as the thing runs, your life has a new focus. The reader, however, is free to come and go. The poet has to stay. The poet is a lifer. Anyone who gets into the game will soon start wishing that there was a version of it with lower stakes, but there isn't.

London, 2008

Opal Sunset

The Book of My Enemy Has Been Remaindered

The book of my enemy has been remaindered
And I am pleased.
In vast quantities it has been remaindered.
Like a van-load of counterfeit that has been seized
And sits in piles in a police warehouse,
My enemy's much-praised effort sits in piles
In the kind of bookshop where remaindering occurs.
Great, square stacks of rejected books and, between them, aisles
One passes down reflecting on life's vanities,
Pausing to remember all those thoughtful reviews
Lavished to no avail upon one's enemy's book –
For behold, here is that book
Among these ranks and banks of duds,
These ponderous and seemingly irreducible cairns
Of complete stiffs.

The book of my enemy has been remaindered
And I rejoice.
It has gone with bowed head like a defeated legion
Beneath the yoke.
What avail him now his awards and prizes,
The praise expended upon his meticulous technique,
His individual new voice?
Knocked into the middle of next week
His brainchild now consorts with the bad buys,
The sinkers, clinkers, dogs and dregs,
The Edsels of the world of movable type,
The bummers that no amount of hype could shift,
The unbudgeable turkeys.

Yea, his slim volume with its understated wrapper
Bathes in the glare of the brightly jacketed *Hitler's War Machine*,
His unmistakably individual new voice
Shares the same scrapyard with a forlorn skyscraper
Of *The Kung-Fu Cookbook*,
His honesty, proclaimed by himself and believed in by others,
His renowned abhorrence of all posturing and pretence,
Is there with *Pertwee's Promenades and Pierrots –*
One Hundred Years of Seaside Entertainment,
And (oh, this above all) his sensibility,
His sensibility and its hair-like filaments,
His delicate, quivering sensibility is now as one
With *Barbara Windsor's Book of Boobs*,
A volume graced by the descriptive rubric
'My boobs will give everyone hours of fun'.

Soon now a book of mine could be remaindered also,
Though not to the monumental extent
In which the chastisement of remaindering has been meted out
To the book of my enemy,
Since in the case of my own book it will be due
To a miscalculated print run, a marketing error –
Nothing to do with merit.
But just supposing that such an event should hold
Some slight element of sadness, it will be offset
By the memory of this sweet moment.
Chill the champagne and polish the crystal goblets!
The book of my enemy has been remaindered
And I am glad.

Sack Artist

Reeling between the redhead and the blonde
Don Juan caught the eye of the brunette.
He had no special mission like James Bond.
He didn't play the lute or read *Le Monde*.
Why was it he on whom their sights were set?

For let's make no mistake, the women pick
Which men go down in history as avid
Tail-chasers with the enviable trick
Of barely needing to chat up the chick –
From Warren Beatty back to ruddy David.

But why the broads latch on to the one bloke
Remains what it has always been, a riddle.
Byron though famous was both fat and broke
While Casanova was a standing joke,
His wig awry, forever on the fiddle.

Mozart made Juan warble but so what?
In *Don Giovanni* everybody sings.
The show would fall flat if the star did not
And clearly he's not meant to sound so hot:
His women praise him, but for other things.

They trill of his indifference and disdain
But might have liked his loyalty still more.
We can't, from how they lyrically complain,
Conclude that when he left they liked the pain
As much as they enjoyed the bliss before.

Bad treatment doesn't do it: not from him,
Still less from us, who find out when we try it
That far from looking tickled they turn grim,
Leaving us at a loss out on a limb,
Instructed to obtain a kite and fly it.

Which doesn't make the chap of whom we speak
Some gigolo devoted to their pleasure.
The fancy man turns no strong woman weak
But merely pumps out what was up the creek.
Plundering hulks he lays up little treasure.

Good looks don't hurt but rate low on their own.
The teenage girls who fall for Richard Gere
Admit his face is random flesh and bone
Beside Mel Gibson's, that his skin lacks tone
And when he smiles his pin eyes disappear.

They go bananas when he bares his chest
But torsos that outstrip his leave them cold.
One bit of you might well be the world's best
But women won't take that and leave the rest:
The man entire is what they would enfold.

The phallus fallacy thus shows its roots
Afloat in the pornographer's wet dream
By which a synechdochic puss in boots
Strides forward frantic to be in cahoots
With his shy mote grown into a great beam.

A shame to be without the wherewithal
But all the wherewith you might have down there
Won't get the ladies queuing in the hall –
Not if you let it loose at a masked ball,
Not if you advertise it on the air.

None of which means that lust takes a back seat.
Contrariwise, it is the main event.
The grandest *grandes dames* cease to be discreet.
Their souls shine through their bodies with the heat.
They dream of more to come as they lie spent.

The sort of women who don't do such things
Do them for him, wherein might lie the clue.
The smell of transcendental sanction clings
Like injured ozone to angelic wings –
An envoy, and he's only passing through.

In triumph's moment he must hit the trail.
However warm the welcome, he can't stay.
Lest those fine fingers read his back like braille
He has to pull out early without fail –
Preserve his mystery with a getaway.

He is the perfect stranger. Humbler grades
Of female don't get even a brief taste –
With Errol Flynn fenced in by flashing blades
And Steve McQueen in aviator shades
It always was a dream that they embraced.

Sheer fantasy makes drama from the drab,
Sweet reverie a slow blues from the bleak:
How Cary Grant would not pick up the tab,
Omar Sharif sent roses in a cab,
Those little lumps in Robert Redford's cheek.

Where Don's concerned the first glance is enough:
For certain he takes soon what we might late.
The rest of us may talk seductive guff
Unendingly and not come up to snuff,
Whereat we most obscenely fulminate.

We say of her that she can't pass a prick.
We call him cunt-struck, stick-man, power tool,
Muff-diver, stud, sack artist, motor dick,
Getting his end away, dipping his wick,
A stoat, a goat, a freak, a fucking fool.

So we stand mesmerised by our own fuss,
Aware that any woman, heaped with grief,
Will give herself to him instead of us
Because there is so little to discuss –
And cry *perfido mostro!* in relief.

Her true desires at long last understood,
She ponders, as she holds him locked above her,
The living definition of the good –
Her blind faith in mankind and womanhood
Restored by the dumb smile of the great lover.

A Gesture towards James Joyce

My gesture towards *Finnegans Wake* is deliberate.
– Ronald Bush, *T. S. Eliot: A Study
in Character and Style*

The gesture towards *Finnegans Wake* was deliberate.
It was not accidental.
Years of training went into the gesture,
As W. C. Fields would practise a juggling routine
Until his eczema-prone hands bled in their kid gloves;
As Douglas Fairbanks Sr trimmed the legs of a table
Until, without apparent effort and from a standing start,
He could jump up on to it backwards;
Or as Gene Kelly danced an entire tracking shot over and over
Until the final knee-slide ended exactly in focus,
Loafers tucked pigeon-toed behind him,
Perfect smile exultant,
Hands thrown open saying 'How *about* that?'

The gesture towards *Finnegans Wake* was deliberate.
Something so elaborate could not have been otherwise.
Though an academic gesture, it partook in its final form
Of the balletic arabesque,
With one leg held out extended to the rear
And the equiponderant forefinger pointing demonstratively
Like the statue of Eros in Piccadilly Circus,
Or, more correctly, the Mercury of Giambologna,
Although fully, needless to say, clad.

The gesture towards *Finnegans Wake* was deliberate,
Its aim assisted by the position of the volume,
A 1957 printing in the yellow and orange wrapper
Propped on a sideboard and opened at page 164
So that the gesture might indicate a food-based conceit
About *pudding the carp before doeuvre hors* –
The Joycean amalgam in its ludic essence,
Accessible to students and yet also evincing
The virtue of requiring a good deal of commentary
Before what looked simple even if capricious
Emerged as precise even if complex
And ultimately unfathomable.

The gesture towards *Finnegans Wake* was deliberate,
Being preceded by an 'It is no accident, then',
An exuberant 'It is neither accidental nor surprising'
And at least two cases of 'It is not for nothing that',
These to adumbrate the eventual paroxysm
In the same way that a bouncer from Dennis Lillee
Has its overture of giant strides galumphing towards you
With the face both above and below the ridiculous moustache
Announcing by means of unmistakable grimaces
That what comes next is no mere spasm
But a premeditated attempt to knock your block off.

The gesture towards *Finnegans Wake* was deliberate
And so was my gesture with two fingers.
In America it would have been one finger only
But in Italy I might have employed both arms,
The left hand crossing to the tense right bicep
As my clenched fist jerked swiftly upwards –
The most deliberate of all gestures because most futile,
Defiantly conceding the lost battle.

The gesture towards *Finnegans Wake* was deliberate:
So much so that Joyce should have seen it coming.
Even through the eyepatch of his last years.
He wrote a book full of nothing except writing
For people who can't do anything but read,
And now their gestures clog the air around us.
He asked for it, and we got it.

Thoughts on Feeling Carbon-Dated

No moons are left to see the other side of.
Curved surfaces betray once secret centres.
Those plagues were measles the Egyptians died of.
A certain note of disillusion enters.

Were Empson starting now, no doubt exists
That now no doubt exists about space-time's
Impetuosity, his pithy gists
Would still stun, but no more so than his rhymes.

Physics has dished its prefix meta. Science,
First having put black shoes and a blue suit on,
Controls the world's supply of mental giants.
A Goethe now would lack words to loathe Newton.

It's forty years since James Joyce named the quark.
Now nobody's nonplussed to hear light rays
Get sucked down holes so fast they show up dark.
Nor would the converse of that news amaze.

It all gets out of reach as it grows clear.
What we once failed to grasp but still were thrilled with
Left us for someone else, from whom we hear
Assurances about the awe they're filled with.

One night in Cambridge Empson read to us.
He offered us some crisps and seemed delighted
So many young should still want to discuss
Why science once got laymen so excited.

Johnny Weissmuller Dead in Acapulco

Apart possibly from waving hello to the cliff-divers
Would the real Tarzan have ever touched Acapulco?
Not with a one-hundred-foot vine.
Jungle Jim maybe, but the Ape Man never.
They played a tape at his funeral
In the Valley of Light cemetery of how he had sounded
Almost fifty years back giving the pristine ape-call,
Which could only remind all present that in decline
He would wander distractedly in the garden
With his hands to his mouth and the unforgettable cry
Coming out like a croak –
This when he wasn't sitting in his swim-trunks
Beside the pool he couldn't enter without nurses.

Things had not been so bad before Mexico
But they were not great.
He was a greeter in Caesar's Palace like Joe Louis.
Sal, I want you should meet Johnny Weissmuller.
Johnny, Mr Sal Volatile is a friend of ours from Chicago.
With a dozen Tarzan movies behind him
Along with the five Olympic gold medals,
He had nothing in front except that irrepressible paunch
Which brought him down out of the tree house
To earth as Jungle Jim
So a safari suit could cover it up.
As Jungle Jim he wasn't just on salary,
He had a piece of the action,
But coming so late in the day it was not enough
And in Vegas only the smile was still intact.

As once it had all been intact, the Greek classic body
Unleashing the new-style front-up crawl like a baby
Lifting itself for the first time,
Going over the water almost as much as through it,
Curing itself of childhood polio
By making an aquaplane of its deep chest,
Each arm relaxing out of the water and stiffening into it,
The long legs kicking a trench that did not fill up
Until he came back on the next lap,
Invincible, easily breathing
The air in the spit-smooth, headlong, creek-around-a-rock
       trough
Carved by his features.

He had six wives like Henry VIII but don't laugh,
Because Henry VIII couldn't swim a stroke
And if you ever want to see a true king you should watch
       Weissmuller
In *Tarzan Escapes* cavorting underwater with Boy
In the clear river with networks of light on the shelving sand
Over which they fly weightless to hide from each other behind
       the log
While Jane wonders where they are.
You will wonder where you are too and be shy of the answer
Because it is Paradise.

When the crocodile made its inevitable entry into the clear river
Tarzan could always settle its hash with his bare hands
Or a knife at most,
But Jungle Jim usually had to shoot it
And later on he just never got to meet it face to face –
It was working for the Internal Revenue Service.

There was a chimpanzee at his funeral,
Which must have been someone's idea of a smart promotion,
And you might say dignity had fled,
But when Tarzan dropped from the tall tree and swam out of
      the splash
Like an otter with an outboard to save Boy from the waterfall
It looked like poetry to me,
And at home in the bath I would surface giving the ape-call.

Will Those Responsible Come Forward?

May the Lord have mercy on all those peoples
Who suffer from a perversion of religion –
Or, to put it in a less equivocating way,
Who suffer from an excess of religion –
Or, to come right out with it,
Who suffer from religion.

Let Him tell those catholic Protestants or protestant Catholics
Who in Northern Ireland go to bed on Saturday night
Looking forward to a morning of Holy Worship
That just this once they should make other plans –
Have a heavy cold, a stomach upset or a pulled hamstring
Severe enough to render them immobile,
With something similar for their children –
So that they will not be there to form a congregation
In a church just big enough for a small massacre.
Arrange this reprieve, Lord,
And if you can't manage that much then for Christ's sake
Hand the whole deal over to Allah.

May the Lord with the assistance of Allah
Give heed to the cries of those children in Beirut
Who have the dubious luck to be ten years old and under
While dwelling in the vicinity of a PLO faction
Currently being wiped out by another PLO faction,
And kindly swing it so that the incoming rockets
Do not dismember their small persons irreparably.
Children older than ten years we will give up on,
Not wanting the moon,
And their mothers, needless to say, are for the high jump.

Fix it, Lord. Get Al on to it,
And if it turns out to be more than you can handle
Raise Jehovah on the horn.

May the Lord and Allah with Jehovah's proverbial
In-depth back-up and sales apparatus
Make a concerted effort to cut the crap,
For the following reasons among others:

Lest at least two kinds of Christians during their annual shoot-out
Bisect an old lady who hears the word 'Duck!'
But can't hit the deck because of sciatica
(May her stoop be steep) –

Lest the Druze and the Jews or the Juze and the Drews,
When shelling each other from somewhere each side
Of a ridge or a bridge,
Cascade hot shrapnel on the intervening hospital
Whose patients suffer from mental disorders,
And thus exacerbate in those inherently unstable minds
An already acute sense of insecurity
(May their straitjackets be flak jackets) –

Lest Iraq and Iran or Iran and Iraq go to rack and ruin
Not just in the standard Islamic manner
Of finding each other insufficiently fanatical,
But with an ironic new wrinkle
By which the hitherto unapproachably sordid
Ayatollah or Arsola
Is upstaged by his own appointee,
That even more sadistic fuckwit and fruitcake
The Hayula or Payola,
Who has women tortured in front of their husbands

As a forceful reminder, no doubt supererogatory,
That you can't fight central mosque
(May their screams be deafening) –

Who also, if that doesn't do the trick,
Has the children tortured along with their mothers
(May they all go crazy quickly),
The object being to make the fathers admit
That they plotted the regime's overthrow –
A pretty fantastic charge when you consider
That the regime's overthrow hasn't yet been accomplished
By Allah functioning either on his tod
Or in combination with the Lord, Jehovah,
Buddha, the Great Spirit and each and every other
Recognized form of God –

Always supposing that They are working on it.
Always supposing that They care
About that or anything else.

But this is the sin of despair.

Echo Echo Echo

Changes in temperature entail turmoil.
Petits pois palpitate before they boil.
Ponds on the point of freezing look like oil.
And God knows what goes on below the soil.

God and the naturalists, who penetrate
With camera crews to depths as dark as fate
And shoot scenes hideous to contemplate
Where burrowing Attenboroughs fight and mate.

In outer space the endless turbulence
Seems too far gone to be at our expense.
One likes to think that if a bang's immense
It didn't happen in the present tense.

Still it's unnerving when two galaxies –
One Catherine wheel and one like a Swiss cheese –
Get stuck in with sharp elbows and scraped knees,
Cancelling out their twin eternities.

As for inside the atom here at home,
It makes the cosmos look like *jeu de paume*
Played out around the Houston Astrodome.
We might as well be back in ancient Rome.

Random, unjust and violent universe!
We feel, and those less ignorant feel worse,
Knowing that what's observed must soon disperse
And Phaethon's car turn out to be a hearse.

Hence, or despite that, our concern with form,
Though even here outclassed by nature's norm.
Snowflakes knock spots off Philibert de L'Orme
But something tells us that they are not warm.

Not that *we* are, compared with, say, the worms
Who live on lava, or are those the germs
That breed in butane and eat isotherms?
I'm not much good with scientific terms.

Even for Einstein it remained a dream
To unify the field, which makes it seem
Likely the rest of us won't get a gleam
Of how, or if, the whole works fit a scheme.

One merely hopes that we have made a start.
Our apprehensions might not melt the heart
Or even be heartfelt for the most part,
But from that insufficiency comes art.

We gather ourselves up from the abyss
As lovers after copulation kiss –
Lip-service which, while semaphoring bliss,
Puts in a claim that there was point to this.

Small wonder, therefore, that from time to time,
As dollar millionaires still nickel-and-dime,
The free-form poet knuckles down to rhyme –
Scared into neatness by the wild sublime.

The Anchor of the *Sirius*

Triangular Macquarie Place, up from the Quay,
Is half rainforest, half a sculpture park
Where can be found – hemmed in by palms and ferns,
Trees touching overhead – the Obelisk
From which, one learns, All Public Roads are Measured
Leading to the Interior of the Colony.
Skyscraper cliffs keep this green garden dark.

The Obelisk is sandstone. Thomas Mort
Is also present, bronze on a tall plinth –
His plain Victorian three-piece suit bulks large,
Befitting Sydney's first successful exporter
Of refrigerated foods – while, lower down
This plush declivity, one finds a bubbler
Superfluously shaded by a small
But intricate gun-metal *baldacchino*,
Sure-footed as a Donatello font.

Thus in a sculpture court less up to date
Yet cooler than MOMA's, leafier than the Frick,
One strolls encountering pieces carried out
In traditional materials and is lulled –
Till this free-standing object looms and startles
Like a Calder by Duchamp. It stops you cold,
The anchor of the *Sirius*. It hooks you
More firmly than the fluke which can't be seen
(Because, presumably, buried in the earth)
Could ever have snared the bottom of Sydney Cove.

One is amazed by how it is not old –
Which means the Colony's protracted birth
(The women were outscreamed by the flayed men)
Falls so far short of being long ago
It's hard to grasp. The anchor was brought back
From where the ship ended its history –
I think it tried to sail through Norfolk Island –
To where it began ours. Yes, the First Fleet
Dropped its first anchor just one hundred yards
(Or metres, as they say now) down the street –
And this is it, not much more touched by time
Than now by me, a yokel in the museum.

The crops failed. Phillip was no dynamo,
But Macquarie was, and men like Mort could double
The town's wealth in ten years. The scrub grew long
And lush like Joan Sutherland's throat. Success
Went overseas, took umpteen curtain calls,
Was toasted and had toast named after it,
And now the audience is here. Out on the harbour
Captain Cook II jam-packed with Japanese,
Their Nikons crackling like automatic flak,
Goes swanning past the well-remembered line
Where the submarine nets were when I was young,
Forty years ago – i.e. a full
Fifth of the time Port Jackson's had that name.

And after I'd grown up and gone away
Like the wool-clip to the other end of the world
(Where the wool was turned to suit-cloth and sent back
So Thomas Mort, full of ideas as Dickens,
Might look the part of the philanthropist)
The anchor of the *Sirius* had me pinned –
Spiked, rooted to the spot under these trees
Which filter what light's left by the glass towers
They put up yesterday so that the banks –
Algemene Bank Nederland NV,
Dresdner Bank AG, Banco Nazionale del Lavoro,
Sumitomo International Finance Australia –
Might catch through tinted windows like hot news
Digits conveying all they need to know,
Drawn down from space by ranks of VDUs
And here made manifest as a green glow –
New York and London, Hong Kong, Tokyo,
Sucked in at once to this same lightning rod –
Completing their great journey from afar
As a tired sinner comes at last to God,
As a ship comes in and drops anchor.

The Ferry Token

Not gold but some base alloy, it stays good
For one trip though the currency inflates –
Hard like the ferry's deck of seasoned wood,
The only coin in town that never dates.

Don Juan, as described by Baudelaire,
Before he crossed the Styx to the grim side
Paid Charon *son obole*, his ferry fare.
Was it this very token, worth one ride?

Of course it wasn't. This poor thing will buy
The traveller no myth beyond the dark
Leonine Pinchgut with one beady eye
Fixed on the brilliant, beckoning Luna Park.

At most it takes you back to Billy Blue
Whose ferry linked the Quay to the North Shore
Somewhere about the year of Waterloo –
And probably more after than before.

There's been so little time for grand events.
One ferry sank, but saying those who drowned
Contributed to our historic sense
Would be obscene and logically unsound.

Nevertheless nostalgia impregnates
This weightless disc as sunlight bleaches wood.
Our past is shallow but it scintillates –
Not gold but some base alloy, it stays good.

A Valediction for Philip Larkin

You never travelled much but now you have,
Into the land whose brochures you liked least:
That drear Bulgaria beyond the grave
Where wonders have definitively ceased –
Ranked as a dead loss even in the East.

Friends will remember until their turn comes
What they were doing when the news came through.
I landed in Nairobi with eardrums
Cracked by the flight from Kichwa Tembo. You
Had gone, I soon learned, on safari too.

Learned soon but too late, since no telephone
Yet rings in the wild country where we'd been.
No media penetration. On one's own
One wakes up and unzips the morning scene
Outside one's tent and always finds it green.

Green Hills of Africa, wrote Hemingway.
Omitting a preliminary 'the',
He made the phrase more difficult to say –
The hills, however, easier to see,
Their verdure specified initially.

Fifty years on, the place still packs a thrill.
Several reserves of greenery survive,
And now mankind may look but must not kill
Some animals might even stay alive,
Surrounded by attentive four-wheel-drive

Toyotas full of tourists who shoot rolls
Of colour film off in the cheetah's face
While she sleeps in the grass or gravely strolls
With bloody cheeks back from the breathless chase,
Alone except for half the human race.

But we patrolled a less well-beaten trail.
Making a movie, we possessed the clout
To shove off up green hill and down green dale
And put our personal safety in some doubt
By opening the door and getting out.

Thus I descended on the day you died
And had myself filmed failing to get killed.
A large male lion left me petrified
But well alone and foolishly fulfilled,
Feeling weak-kneed but calling it strong-willed.

Silk brushed with honey in the hot noon light,
His inside leg was colonized by flies.
I made a mental note though wet with fright.
As his mouth might have done off me, my eyes
Tore pieces off him to metabolize.

In point of fact I swallowed Kenya whole,
A mill choked by a plenitude of grist.
Like anabolic steroids for the soul,
Every reagent was a catalyst –
So much to take in sent me round the twist.

I saw Kilimanjaro like the wall
Of Heaven going straight up for three miles.
The Mara river was a music hall
With tickled hippos rolling in the aisles.
I threw some fast food to the crocodiles.

I chased giraffes who floated out of reach
Like anglepoise lamps loose in zero g.
I chased a *mdudu* with a can of bleach
Around my tent until I couldn't see.
Only a small rhinoceros chased me.

The spectral sun-bird drew the mountain near,
And if the rain-bird singing *soon soon soon*
Turned white clouds purple, still the air was clear –
The radiant behind of a baboon
Was not more opulent than the full moon.

So one more tourist should have been agog
At treasure picked up cheaply while away –
Ecstatic as some latter-day sea dog,
His trolley piled high like a wain of hay
With duty-free goods looted from Calais.

For had I not enlarged my visual scope,
Perhaps my whole imaginative range,
By seeing how that deadpan antelope,
The topi, stands on small hills looking strange
While waiting for the traffic lights to change?

And had I not observed the elephant
Deposit heaps of steaming excrement
While looking wiser than Immanuel Kant,
More stately than the present Duke of Kent?
You start to see why I was glad I went.

Such sights were trophies, ivory and horn
Destined for carving into *objets d'art*.
Ideas already jumping like popcorn,
I climbed down but had not gone very far
Between that old Dakota and the car

When what they told me stretched the uncrossed space
Into a universe. No tears were shed.
Forgive me, but I hardly felt a trace
Of grief. Just sudden fear your being dead
So soon had left us disinherited.

You were the one who gave us the green light
To get out there and seek experience,
Since who could equal you at sitting tight
Until the house around you grew immense?
Your bleak bifocal gaze was so intense,

Hull stood for England, England for the world –
The whole caboodle crammed into one room.
Above your desk all of creation swirled
For you to look through with increasing gloom,
Or so your poems led us to assume.

Yet even with your last great work 'Aubade'
(To see death clearly, did you pull it close?)
The commentator must be on his guard
Lest he should overlook the virtuose
Technique which makes majestic the morose.

The truth is that you revelled in your craft.
Profound glee charged your sentences with wit.
You beat them into stanza form and laughed:
They didn't sound like poetry one bit,
Except for being absolutely it.

Described in English written at its best
The worst of life remains a bitch to face
But is more shared, which leaves us less depressed –
Pleased the condition of the human race,
However desperate, is touched with grace.

The seeming paradox is a plain fact –
You brought us all together on your own.
Your saddest lyric is a social act.
A bedside manner in your graveyard tone
Suggests that at the last we aren't alone.

You wouldn't have agreed, of course. You said
Without equivocation that life ends
With him who lived it definitely dead
And buried, after which event he tends
To spend a good deal less time with his friends.

But you aren't here to argue. Where you are
By now is anybody's guess but yours.
I'm five miles over Crete in a Tristar
Surrounded by the orchestrated snores
Induced by some old film of Roger Moore's.

Things will be tougher now you've proved your point,
By leaving early, that the man upstairs
Neither controls what happens in the joint
We call the world, nor noticeably cares.
While being careful not to put on airs,

It is perhaps the right time to concede
That life is all downhill from here on in.
For doing justice to it, one will need,
If not in the strict sense a sense of sin,
More *gravitas* than fits into a grin.

But simply staying put makes no one you.
Those who can't see the world in just one street
Must see the world. What else is there to do
Except face inescapable defeat
Flat out in a first-class reclining seat?

You heard the reaper in the Brynmor Jones
Library cough behind your swivel chair.
I had to hear those crocodiles crunch bones,
Like cars compressed for scrap, before the hair
Left on my head stood straight up in the air.

You saw it all in little. You dug deep.
A lesser man needs coarser stimuli,
Needs coruscating surfaces . . . needs sleep.
I'm very rarely conscious when I fly.
Not an event in life. To sleep. To die.

I wrote that much, then conked out over Rome,
Dreamed I'd been sat on by a buffalo,
Woke choking as we tilted down for home,
And now see, for once cloudless, the pale glow
Of evening on the England you loved so

And spoke for in a way she won't forget.
The quiet voice whose resonance seemed vast
Even while you lived, and which has now been set
Free by the mouth that shaped it shutting fast,
Stays with us as you turn back to the past –

Your immortality complete at last.

Jet Lag in Tokyo

Flat feet kept Einstein out of the army.
The Emperor's horse considers its position.
In Akasaka men sit down and weep
Because the night must end.

At Chez Oz I discussed my old friend's sex change
With a lovely woman who, I later learned,
Had also had one. The second movement
Of the Mahler Seventh on my Boodo Kahn
Above the North Pole spoke to me like you.

Neutrinos from 1987A
Arrived in the Kamikande bubble chamber
Three hours before the light. Shinjuku neon
Is dusted with submicroscopic diamonds.

Our belled cat keeps blackbirds up to scratch
With the fierce face of a tiger from the wall
Of the Ko-hojo in the Nanzen-ji, Kyoto.
You would not have been looking for me,
God told Pascal,
If you had not found me.

What will we do with those Satsuma pots
When the sun dies? Our Meissen *vieux Saxe* girl
Was fired three times. The car will be OK:
A Volkswagen can take anything.

An age now since I wrote about your beauty,
How rare it is. Tonight I am reminded.
Sue-Ellen Ewing says *Gomen nasai*.
Perhaps the Emperor's horse is awake also.
I think this time I've gone too far too fast.

What Happened to Auden

His stunning first lines burst out of the page
Like a man thrown through a windscreen. His flat drawl
Was acrid with the spirit of the age –
The spy's last cigarette, the hungry sprawl
Of Hornby clockwork train sets in 'O' gauge,
Huge whitewashed slogans on a factory wall –
It was as if a spotlight when he spoke
Brilliantly pierced the histrionic smoke.

Unsentimental as the secret police,
Contemporary as a Dinky Toy,
On holiday in Iceland with MacNeice,
A flop-haired Cecil Beaton golden boy,
Auden pronounced like Pericles to Greece
The short time Europe had left to enjoy,
Yet made it sound as if impending doom
Could only ventilate the drawing room.

Splendidly poised above the ashtray's rim,
The silver record-breaking aeroplane
For streamlined utterance could not match him.
Oblique but no more often than the rain,
Impenetrable only to the dim,
Neurotic merely not to be insane,
He seemed to make so much sense all at once
Anyone puzzled called himself a dunce.

Cricket pavilion lust looked a touch twee
Even to devotees, but on the whole,
Apart from harsh reviews in *Scrutiny*,
All hailed his triumph in Cassandra's role,
Liking the *chic* he gave her, as if she
Wore ankle-strap high heels and a mink stole –
His ambiguity just further proof
Here was a man too proud to stand aloof.

By now, of course, we know he was in fact
As queer as a square grape, a roaring queen
Himself believing the forbidden act
Of love he made a meal of was obscene.
He could be crass and generally lacked tact.
He had no truck with personal hygiene.
The roughest trade would seldom stay to sleep.
In soiled sheets he was left alone to weep.

From the Kurfürstendamm to far Shanghai
He cruised in every sense with Isherwood.
Sadly he gave the talent the glad eye
And got out while the going was still good.
New York is where his genius went to die
Say those who disapproved, but though they could
Be right that he lost much of his allure,
Whether this meant decline is not so sure.

Compatriots who stuck it out have said
Guilt for his getaway left him unmanned,
Whereat his taproot shrivelled and went dead,
Having lost contact with its native land.
Some say it was the sharing of his bed
With the one man nobody else could stand
That did him in, since poets can't afford
The deadly risk of conjugal concord.

But Chester made bliss hard enough to take,
And Wystan, far from pining for his roots,
Gaily tucked into the unrationed steak.
An international figure put out shoots.
Stravinsky helped the progress of the rake:
Two cultural nabobs were in cahoots.
No, Auden ageing was as much at home
On the world stage as Virgil was in Rome,

If less than *salonfähig* still. Regret
By all accounts he sparingly displayed
When kind acquaintances appeared upset,
Their guest rooms wrecked as if by an air raid.
He would forgive himself and soon forget.
Pig-like he revelled in the mess he made,
Indecorous the more his work lost force,
Devoid of shame. Devoured, though, by remorse,

For had he not gazed into the abyss
And found, as Nietzsche warned, that it gazed back?
His wizardry was puerile next to this.
No spark of glamour touched the railway track
That took whole populations to the hiss
Of cyanide and stoked the chimney stack
Scattering ash above a vast expanse
Of industry bereft of all romance.

The pit cooled down but still he stood aghast
At how far he had failed to state the case
With all those tricks that now seemed so half-arsed.
The inconceivable had taken place.
Waking to find his wildest dreams outclassed
He felt his tongue must share in the disgrace,
And henceforth be confined, in recompense,
To no fine phrase devoid of plain prose sense.

The bard unstrung his lyre to change his tune,
Constrained his inspiration to repent.
Dry as the wind abrading a sand dune,
A tightly drafted letter of intent,
Each rubric grew incisive like a rune,
Merest suggestions became fully meant.
The ring of truth was in the level tone
He forged to fit hard facts and praise limestone.

His later manner leaves your neck-hair flat,
Not standing up as Housman said it should
When poetry has been achieved. For that,
In old age Auden simply grew too good.
A mortal fear of talking through his hat,
A moral mission to be understood
Precisely, made him extirpate the thrill
Which, being in his gift, was his to kill.

He wound up as a poor old fag at bay,
Beleaguered in the end as at the start
By dons appalled that he could talk all day
And not draw breath although pissed as a fart,
But deep down he had grown great, in a way
Seen seldom in the history of his art –
Whose earthly limits Auden helped define
By realising he was not divine.

Last Night the Sea Dreamed It Was Greta Scacchi

Last night the sea dreamed it was Greta Scacchi.
It wakes unruffled, lustrous, feeling sweet –
Not one breath of scandal has ever touched it.

At a higher level, the rain has too much power.
Grim clouds conspire to bring about its downfall.
The squeeze is on, there is bound to be a shake-out.

The smug sea and the sky that will soon go bust
Look like antagonists, but don't be fooled:
They understand each other very well.

We are caught between the hammer and the anvil.
Our bodies, being umpteen per cent water,
Are in this thing up to the neck at least.

If you want to feel detached from a panorama,
Try the Sahara. Forget about Ayers Rock –
The sea was once all over it like a rash.

The water in the opal makes it lovely,
Also unlucky. If not born in October
You might be wearing a cloudburst for a pendant.

The ban on flash photography is lifted.
The reception area expectantly lights up.
No contest. It's just life. Don't try to fight it –

You'll only get wet through, and we are that
Already. Every dimple in the swell
Is a drop in the ocean, but then who isn't?

No, nothing about women is more sensual
Than their sea smell. Look at her lying there,
Taking what comes and spreading it on her skin –

The cat, she's using her cream as moisturizer.
Milt Jackson's mallets bounce on silver leaves.
Strafed by cool riffs she melts in silent music:

Once we walked out on her, but we'll be back.

Drama in the Soviet Union

When Kaganovich, brother-in-law of Stalin,
Left the performance barely halfway through,
Meyerhold must have known that he was doomed,
Yet ran behind the car until he fell.
In *Pravda* he'd been several times condemned
For Stubborn Formalism. The ill will
Of the All Highest himself was common knowledge,
Proved by a mud slide of denunciations
And rubbed in by the fact that the Great Teacher
Had never personally entered the theatre
Which this enemy of the people had polluted
With attitudes hostile to the State.

Thus Meyerhold was a dead man of long standing:
Behind the big black car it was a corpse
That ran, a skull that gasped for air,
Bare bone that flailed and then collapsed.
His dear friend Shostakovich later said
How glad he was that he had never seen
Poor Meyerhold like that. Which was perhaps
Precisely why this giant of his art
Did such a thing: to dramatize the fear
Which had already eaten him alive
And make it live.

                    Stalin, meanwhile,
Who didn't need to see how it was done
To know that the director's trick of staging
A scene so it could never be forgotten
Had to be stamped on, was the acknowledged master
Of the one theatrical effect that mattered –
He knew how to make people disappear.
So Meyerhold, having limped home, plummeted
Straight through the trapdoor to oblivion.
Nobody even registered surprise.
Specific memories were not permitted.
People looked vague, as if they didn't have them.
In due course his widow, too, was murdered –
Stabbed in the eyes, allegedly by thieves.

Budge Up

Flowering cherry pales to brush-stroke pink at blossom fall
Like watermelon bitten almost to the rind.
It is in his mind because the skin is just that colour
Hot on her tight behind
As she lies in the bath, a Bonnard flipped like a flapjack.

His big black towel turns a naiad to a dryad,
No pun intended. Then,
An unwrapped praline,
She anoints herself with liberal Oil of Ulay.
It looks like fun.
Her curved fingers leave a few streaks not rubbed in.
He says: here, let me help.

The night is young but not as young as she is
And he is older than the hills.
Sweet sin
Swallows him at a gulp.

While cherry blossom suds dry on the lawn
Like raspberry soda
He attends the opening of the blue tulip
Mobbed at the stage door by forget-me-nots.

For a short season
He basks in her reflected glory.

Pathetic fallacy,
Dispelled by the clattering plastic rake.

Bring Me the Sweat of Gabriela Sabatini

Bring me the sweat of Gabriela Sabatini
For I know it tastes as pure as Malvern water,
Though laced with bright bubbles like the *aqua minerale*
That melted the kidney stones of Michelangelo
As sunlight the snow in spring.

Bring me the sweat of Gabriela Sabatini
In a green Lycergus cup with a sprig of mint,
But add no sugar –
The bitterness is what I want.
If I craved sweetness I would be asking you to bring me
The tears of Annabel Croft.

I never asked for the wristbands of Maria Bueno,
Though their periodic transit of her glowing forehead
Was like watching a bear's tongue lap nectar.
I never asked for the blouse of Françoise Durr,
Who refused point-blank to improve her soufflé serve
For fear of overdeveloping her upper arm –
Which indeed remained delicate as a fawn's femur,
As a fern's frond under which cool shadows gather
So that the dew lingers.

Bring me the sweat of Gabriela Sabatini
And give me credit for having never before now
Cried out with longing.
Though for all the years since TV acquired colour
To watch Wimbledon for even a single day
Has left me shaking with grief like an ex-smoker
Locked overnight in a cigar factory,
Not once have I let loose as now I do
The parched howl of deprivation,
The croak of need.

Did I ever demand, as I might well have done,
The socks of Tracy Austin?
Did you ever hear me call for the cast-off Pumas
Of Hana Mandlikova?
Think what might have been distilled from these things,
And what a small request it would have seemed –
It would not, after all, have been like asking
For something so intimate as to arouse suspicion
Of mental derangement.
I would not have been calling for Carling Bassett's knickers
Or the tingling, Teddy Tinling B-cup brassière
Of Andrea Temesvari.

Yet I denied myself.
I have denied myself too long.
If I had been Pat Cash at that great moment
Of triumph, I would have handed back the trophy
Saying take that thing away
And don't let me see it again until
It spills what makes this lawn burst into flower:
Bring me the sweat of Gabriela Sabatini.

In the beginning there was Gorgeous Gussie Moran
And even when there was just her it was tough enough,
But by now the top hundred boasts at least a dozen knockouts
Who make it difficult to keep one's tongue
From lolling like a broken roller blind.
Out of deference to Billie-Jean I did my best
To control my male chauvinist urges –
An objectivity made easier to achieve
When Betty Stove came clumping out to play
On a pair of what appeared to be bionic legs
Borrowed from Six Million Dollar Man.

I won't go so far as to say I harbour
Similar reservations about Steffi Graf –
I merely note that her thigh muscles when tense
Look interchangeable with those of Boris Becker –
Yet all are agreed that there can be no doubt
About Martina Navratilova:
Since she lent her body to Charles Atlas
The definition of the veins on her right forearm
Looks like the Mississippi river system
Photographed from a satellite,
And though she may unleash a charming smile
When crouching to dance at the ball with Ivan Lendl,
I have always found to admire her yet remain detached
Has been no problem.

But when the rain stops long enough for the true beauties
To come out swinging under the outshone sun,
The spectacle is hard for a man to take,
And in the case of this supernally graceful dish –
Likened to a panther by slavering sports reporters
Who pitiably fail to realise that any panther
With a topspin forehand line drive like hers
Would be managed personally by Mark McCormack –
I'm obliged to admit defeat.

So let me drink deep from the bitter cup.
Take it to her between any two points of a tie-break
That she may shake above it her thick black hair,
A nocturne from which the droplets as they fall
Flash like shooting stars –
And as their lustre becomes liqueur
Let the full calyx be repeatedly carried to me.
Until I tell you to stop,
Bring me the sweat of Gabriela Sabatini.

Go Back to the Opal Sunset

Go back to the opal sunset, where the wine
Costs peanuts, and the avocado mousse
Is thick and strong as cream from a jade cow.
Before the passion fruit shrinks on the vine
Go back to where the heat turns your limbs loose.
You've worked your heart out and need no excuse.
Knock out your too-tall tent pegs and go now.

It's England, April, and it's pissing down,
So realise your assets and go back
To the opal sunset. Even autumn there
Will swathe you in a raw-silk dressing gown,
And through the midnight harbour lacquered black
The city lights strike like a heart attack
While eucalyptus soothes the injured air.

Now London's notion of a petty crime
Is simple murder or straightforward rape
And Oxford Street's a bombing range, to go
Back to the opal sunset while there's time
Seems only common sense. Make your escape
To where the prawns assume a size and shape
Less like a newborn baby's little toe.

Your tender nose anointed with zinc cream,
A sight for sore eyes will be brought to you.
Bottoms bisected by a piece of string
Will wobble through the heat-haze like a dream
That summer afternoon you go back to
The opal sunset, and it's all as true
As sandfly bite or jelly-blubber sting.

What keeps you here? Is it too late to tell?
It might be something you can't now define,
Your nature altered as if by the moon.
Yet out there at this moment, through the swell,
The hydrofoil draws its triumphant line.
Such powers of decision should be mine.
Go back to the opal sunset. Do it soon.

The Eternity Man

Never filmed, he was photographed only once,
Looking up startled into the death-trap flash
Like a threatened life form.
Still underlining his copybook one-word message
With the flourish that doubled back under the initial 'E',
He was caught red-eyed with the stark white chalk in his hand
Writing Eternity.

Before he died in 1967
At the age of eighty-eight
He had managed to write it five hundred thousand times,
And always in copperplate script.
Few streets or public places in the city of Sydney
Remained unmarked by the man with a single obsession –
Writing Eternity.

Wherever you lived, sooner or later he'd reach you.
Hauling their billycarts up for the day's first run
Small boys swarmed when they came to the word
Arrestingly etched in the footpath.
It was self-protected by its perfect calligraphy –
The scrupulous sweep of a hand that had spent its lifetime
Writing Eternity.

He was born in a Balmain slum and raised underneath it,
Sleeping on hessian bags with his brothers and sisters
To keep beyond fist's reach of his dipso parents.
His name was Arthur Stace.
He had no one to use it apart from his family.
His fate was to die as a man and return as a portent,
Writing Eternity.

His sisters grew up to be prostitutes. He was a pimp,
But in 1930, in his early forties, on meths,
He heard the Reverend John Ridley at Burton Street
Baptist Church, Darlinghurst,
And scrapped his planned night in the down-and-out sanctuary.
The piss artist had his vocation revealed unto him –
Writing Eternity.

'I wish I could shout one word through the streets of Sydney!'
The Reverend Ridley shouted. 'Eternity! You
Have got to meet it! You! Where will you spend
Eternity?' Alone in his pew,
Avoided by all for his smell strong enough to see,
A man reborn saw the path stretch ahead he would stoop to,
Writing Eternity.

In New South Wales for more than a hundred years
We all had to learn that script in school,
But what school did he ever go to, and where
Did his chalk come from? How did he eat?
These nagging conundrums were mulled over endlessly
As he roamed unseen through the city without rhyme or reason
Writing Eternity.

In a blaze of glory the Thousand Year Reich was announced.
Old Bolsheviks shyly confessed with downcast eyes
And the first reffos arrived at Woolloomooloo.
Our troops sailed off to prop up the Middle East
Until Singapore fell and the Yanks overtipped for a taxi –
Yet still through the blacked-out streets he kept his own schedule
Writing Eternity.

But a mere word was ceasing to hold any terrors.
Belief in the afterlife faded. Where was God
When the Christmas snow came fluttering into the death camps?
Those kindling children, their piles of little shoes,
Condemned Divine Justice past hope of apology:
To rage at the storm and expect it to stop made more sense than
Writing Eternity.

He wrote it on the same night Hitler burned.
He wrote it as the Japanese cities melted
And the tanks rolled into Budapest.
While Sputnik skimmed through the stars he bent to his task
As if we believed there was still any Hell except history,
And Heaven could be rebuilt by one scuttling ratbag
Writing Eternity.

The rain didn't always wash his word away.
He sometimes used more than chalk. Near my place once
I found it fingertip deep in the new white concrete.
It was lined with crimson enamel, a rune punched in
By a branding-iron from space. Down on one knee
I chipped out the paint with my penknife as if I could stop him
Writing Eternity.

He wouldn't have known. He didn't have time to go back,
Not even to visit his real bravura efforts
Which culminated in his famous Australia Square
Incised masterpiece filled with stainless steel.
Some snot-nosed kid with a grudge there would always be,
But he put all that behind him and kept on going,
Writing Eternity.

By the time he died I was half the world away
And when I came back I never gave him a thought.
It was almost fifty years after I unpicked it
That I pondered his word again,
On the dawn of the day when the laughing stock was yours truly
Who would have to go on alone and be caught in the spotlight
Writing Eternity.

From the thirty-third floor of the Regent I looked down naked.
The Opera House was sold out. I was afraid,
But the Harbour was flat calm all the way to the sea,
Its shaped, linked loops flush with silver,
And I suddenly saw what that showpiece of geology
Had really been up to ever since the magma cooled –
Writing Eternity.

That word again, and this time I could read it.
It said your life is on loan from those before you
Who had no chance, and before it is even over
Others will come to judge you, if only by
Forgetting your name; so better than glittering vainly
Would be to bend down in the dark half a million times
Writing Eternity.

Where will we spend it? Nowhere except here.
Life everlasting ends where it begins,
On Earth, but it is present at every moment.
We must seek grace now and not for ourselves alone
Was what that crazed saint meant in his ecstasy –
Since time is always, with chalk made from children's ashes,
Writing Eternity.

Reflections in an Extended Kitchen

Late summer charms the birds out of the trees
On to our lawn, where the cat gets them.
Aware of this but not unmanned, Matisse
Makes the whole room as sexy as the girl.

'Distributed voluptuousness,' he said,
Matching the decor to her lazy gaze.
Just book me on the first flight to Morocco.
You see what I see? Feathers on the grass.

Nothing so sordid in Henri's back yard
Where coloured shapes may touch, but not to crush.
Look at that death trap out there, lined with roses!
We grew a free-fire zone with fertilizer.

Caught on the ground like the Egyptian Air Force
A wrecked bird on its back appears outraged:
It could have been a contender. What a world
Of slam-bang stuff to float one fantasy

Amongst her figured curtains, blobs for flowers,
Lolling unlocked in filmy harem pants!
Where did we see her first? That place they called
Leningrad. She looked like History's cure,

And even he could use that. When he turned
An artful blank back on his wife and child
They were arrested, leaving him to paint
In peace a world with no Gestapo in it –

A dream that came true. Agonies recede,
And if his vision hid harsh facts from him
It sharpens them for us. Best to believe
He served an indispensable ideal:

Douceur de vivre on a heroic scale –
Heaven on Earth, the Land of Oobladee,
Cloud Nine and Shangri-la hooked to the wall
As bolt holes for the brain, square wishing wells.

Suppose that like his brush my pen could speak
Volumes, our cat might stay in shape to pounce,
But only on the arm of that soft chair
You sit in now and where you would lie lulled,

An ageless, in-house *odalisque couchée*
Never to be less languorous than this,
Always dissolving in the air around you
Reality's cruel purr with your sweet whisper –

And nothing would be terrible again,
Nor ever was. The fear that we once felt
For daughters fallen ill or just an hour
Late home: it never happened. That dumb bird
Stayed in its tree and I was true to you.

Simple Stanzas about Modern Masters

If T. S. Eliot and Ezra Pound
Came back to life, again it would be found
One had the gab, the other had the gift
And each looked to the other for a lift.

The Waste Land, had not Pound applied his blue
Pencil, might well have seemed less spanking new.
Pound was a crackpot but that made his critical
Prowess particularly analytical.

Embarrassing, however, there's no doubt:
Increasingly too crass to have about.
While Eliot held discreetly right-wing views
Pound yelled obscenities about the Jews.

For Eliot, the time to cause a stir
Was past, and dignity was *de rigueur*,
But Pound preferred to hang out with the boys
In boots and black shirts who made lots of noise.

For Eliot the war brought veneration:
He seemed to speak for his adopted nation.
When Pound spoke it reminded Mussolini
What it had cost them to lose Toscanini.

Pound wound up in a cage and might have swung
Or died strapped down if he had not been sprung.
A big prize for the *Cantos* saved his neck
Though even he half-guessed they were a wreck.

The rackety campaign in Pound's support
Worked only because Eliot took thought
On how *il miglior fabbro* might best be
Saved for a dignified senility.

His tactic was to let it be inferred
That though he nowadays thought Pound absurd,
The established master and his erstwhile mentor
Were still somehow one creature, like a centaur.

One was the head, the other the hindquarters
(A point made by the more astute reporters)
But few dared to protest at a free pass
For such a well-connected horse's arse.

Pound in his dotage made no spark of sense
But Eliot, still staunch in his defence,
Remembered how it took a cocksure friend
To help unscramble radium from pitchblende.

Pound falling silent, Eliot sat in state.
Though some said what he did was etiolate,
Most regally he'd kept the palace rule –
Never lose sight of what you owe your fool.

Son of a Soldier

My tears came late. I was fifty-five years old
Before I began to cry authentically:
First for the hurt I had done to those I loved,
Then for myself, for what had been done to me
In the beginning, to make my heart so cold.

When the floodgates opened, the flood was not like rain.
With the undammed water came the sad refuse:
The slime, the drowned rats and the bloated corpse
Of the man whose absence had plugged up the sluice
That now gushed junk into my neat domain.

Not older by all that much than my dear daughters
He lay disfiguring a flower bed,
As if by bubbling gas a shallow grave
Of massacre had thrust up one of its dead,
Not to be washed clean by the clearest waters.

I took leave of my wife and knelt beside him
Who could have been my son, though I was his,
And everything he had not come back to tell me
About how everlasting true love is
Was a mouth of mud, so thick did woe betide him.

'Had you come home, I would not be what I am,'
I cried. 'I could have loved my mother less
And not searched for more like her among others,
Parched for a passion undimmed by distress
While you lay deep behind that looming dam.'

The wet earth swallowed him. This time his grave
Was marked: at least I knew now where he was.
I turned to meet her eyes. 'Let me explain,'
I said to her. 'My tears were trapped because
He left me to be tender, strong and brave

Who was none of those things. Inflamed by fright,
The love that he did not return to make
To the first woman I knew and could not help,
Became in me a thirst I could never slake
For one more face transfigured by delight,

Yet needing nothing else. It was a doomed quest
Right from the start, and now it is at an end.
I am too old, too raddled, too ashamed.
Can I stay in your house? I need a friend.'
'So did I,' she said truly. 'But be my guest:

God knows I too have waited wasted years
To have my husband home. Our parents wept
For history. Great events prised them apart,
Not greed, guilt, lies and promises unkept.
Pray they come not too late, these healing tears.'

The house we live in and that man-sized mound
Are a long walk between, yet both are real.
Like family life, his flowers have their weeds
To save them from a sanitised ideal.
I hope this balance holds until the ground

Takes me down, too. But I fear they will go on thronging,
Those pipe-dream sprites who promise a fresh start –
Free, easy furies haunting a cot case
That never lived, or loved, with a whole heart –
Until for one last time I die of longing.

What will I tell her then, in that tattoo
Of the last breath, the last gasp, the death rattle?
The truth: that in my life stolen from him
Whose only legacy was a lost battle,
The one thing that belonged to me was you.

Where the Sea Meets the Desert

Antony and Cleopatra swam at Mersa Matruh
In the clear blue shallows.
Imagine the clean sand, the absence of litter –
No plastic bottles or scraps of styrofoam packing,
No jetsam at all except the occasional corpse
Of a used slave tossed off a galley –
And the shrieks of the dancing Queen as the hero splashed her
While her cheer-squad of ladies-in-waiting giggled on cue,
The eunuchs holding the towels.
With salt in her eyes did she wrinkle the perfect nose
Of which Pascal would later venture the opinion
That had it been shorter (he didn't say by how much)
History would have been different?
They were probably both naked. What a servant saw
Did not count. They might even have boffed each other
Right there at the water's edge like a pair of dolphins
Washed up in the middle of a mad affair,
With her unable to believe the big lunk would ever
Walk away from this, and him in his soul
Fighting to forget that this was R&R
And there was still the war.

There is always the war. The Aussies in Tobruk
Could hear the German bombers at El Adem
Warming up on the airfield
For the five-minute flight that is really the only distance
Between bliss and blitz.
Ears still ringing from kookaburras and whipbirds
Were heckled by Heinkels.
When Antony eyeballed her Coppertone tits and bum
He was looking at Actium.

Shake it, lady.
Shake it for the Afrika Korps.
Where the sea meets the desert there is always,
There is always the war.

The Lions at Taronga

The leaves of Tower Bridge are rigged to open
For any taxi I might chance to catch.
They say that when the ravens leave the Tower

It means they'll use my rain-stained study skylight
As a toilet. I can see Canary Wharf,
A Russian rocket packed around with boosters

Lit up to launch at dawn from Baikonur.
The Blade of Light is cleared for butterflies
To crash-land. When that lens-shaped office block

Is finished it will bend a ray from space
To burn the *Belfast* like a sitting duck.
I've known the NatWest Tower since it was knee-high

To the Barbican, another high-tech know-how
HQ that used to look like the last word.
From my place I can see last words in vistas

As far downriver as the spreading spikes
Of the Dome, some sad bitch of a sea urchin
Losing its battle with a stray Dutch cap

While hot-house pleasure boats leak foreign voices
Like tourist minibuses nose to tail
In the corridors of Buckingham Palace.

Been there, done that. The Queen, she hung one on me.
I've got it in a box. The box to frame
My body will be built here, like as not,

And probably quite soon. I've lived in London
For longer than some people live all told.
Except for the way out, I know it backwards.

So at night when the lions at Taronga
Roar in my memory across the water
I feel the way they must have felt, poor bastards –

Gone in the teeth. The food dead. On display
All day and every day. Sleep in a fortress.
Every familiar walkway leads to strangers.

Dream Me Some Happiness

John Donne, uneasiest of apostates,
Renouncing Rome that he might get ahead
In life, or anyway not wind up dead,
Minus his guts or pressed beneath great weights,

Ascribed his bad faith to his latest flame
As if the fact she could be bent to do
His bidding proved that she would not stay true:
Each kiss a Judas kiss, a double game.

Compared with him, the mental muscle-man,
Successors who declared his numbers rough
Revealed by theirs they found the pace too tough:
The knotty strength that made him hard to scan

Left him renowned for his conceits alone,
Figments unfading as the forms of death
Prescribed for Catholics by Elizabeth –
Tangles of gristle, relics of hair and bone.

Brought back to favour in an anxious time
Attuned to his tormented intellect,
By now he charms us, save in one respect:
Framing his women still looks like a crime.

We foist our fault on her we claim to love
A different way. Pleased to the point of tears,
She tells us that the real world disappears.
Not quite the Donne thing, when push comes to shove:

He wrote betrayal into her delight.
We have a better reason to deceive
Ourselves as we help her help us believe
Life isn't like that: at least, not tonight.

Deckard Was a Replicant

The forms of nature cuff-linked through your life
Bring a sense of what Americans call closure.
The full-blown iris swims in English air
Like the wreckage of an airbag jellyfish
Rinsed by a wave's thin edge at Tamarama:
The same frail blue, the same exhausted sprawl,
The same splendour. Nothing but the poison
Is taken out. In the gallery, that girl
Has the beauty that once gave itself to you
To be turned into marriage, children, houses.
She will give these things to someone else this time.

If this time seems the same time, it's because
It is. The reason she is not for you
Is she already was. Try to remember
What power they have, knowing what sex is for:
Replacing us. The Gainsborough chatelaine
She studies wears a shawl dipped in the hint
Of jacaranda blossoms, yet it might
Remind her of sucked sweets, or the pale veins
Of her own breasts. Setting the Thames on fire,
The tall white-painted training ship from Denmark
Flaunts the brass fittings of the little ferry
That took you as a child to Kirribilli
On its way to Wandsworth, then the Acheron
And Hades. Those gulls that graze the mud
Took sixty years to get here from Bundeena.

At an average speed of forty yards an hour
They hardly moved. It seems you didn't either.
You stood still with your head wrapped in the armour
Of perception's hard-wired interlocking habits.
Ned Kelly was the ghost of Hamlet's father.
Dazzled by lipstick pulped from waratahs,
The smoker coughs, having been born again.

Lucretius the Diver

Things worn out by the lapse of ages tend
Toward the reef, that motley wrecking crew
Of living polyps who, to get ahead,
Climb ruthlessly all over their own dead,
But facts like those Lucretius never knew:
He merely meant we can't long buck the trend
That winds up hard against a watershed.

Horace had godly names for every breeze.
Ovid himself was stiff with sacred stuff.
Virgil talked turkey just once, about bees.
Of ancient wits Lucretius alone,
Without recourse to supernatural guff,
Uncannily forecast the modern tone –
Viewing the world as miracle enough.

Imagine him in Scuba gear, instead
Of whatever kit a Roman poet wore –
To find his fruitful symbol for the grave
Not just inevitable but alive
Would surely suit him down to the sea floor.
Suspended before such a flower-bed
He'd bubble with delight beneath the wave.

The reef, a daughter, and the sea, its mother,
In a long, white-lipped rage with one another
Would shout above him as he hung in space
And saw his intuition had been right:
Under a windswept canopy of lace,
Even down there in that froth-filtered light,
The World of Things is clearly the one place –

Death lives, life dies, and no gods intervene.
It's all so obvious, would be his thought:
But then, it always was, at least to him,
And why the rest of them were quite so dim
On that point is perhaps a theme we ought
To tackle, realising it could mean
Our chances going in are pretty slim

Of drawing comfort from a Golden Age
So lethally haphazard no-one sane
Could contemplate the play of chance was all
There was to life. That took the featherbrain
Lucretius seemed to them, and not the sage
He seems to us, who flinch from his disdain
As he stares seaward at the restless wall

Of ruined waves, the spray that falls like rain.

One Man to Another

Salute me! I have tamed my daughter's face
With hot oil, and my honour has been saved.
It's not to be defied that I have slaved.
She talks a lot less now she knows her place.

Most of her mouth can still move, and one eye
Could stare in hatred if she wanted to.
I'm proud to say her protests have been few
Apart from that absurd initial cry.

That was the evil spirit leaving her.
She really should have dealt with it herself.
She said she'd rather end up on the shelf
Than marry our best choice. What thoughts occur

To girls nowadays! Next they will want a say
In what to wear and when to buy a book.
Here, take your mother's mirror. Take a look.
What have you got in store for me today?

You thought to shake my faith? Well, you have found
My faith shakes you, and will again, I swear,
If you continue with that hang-dog air:
If you continue with that whining sound.

Can't you be grateful we still keep you here?
We could have sent you out there to the dust
Where people fight for every cow-pat crust.
We don't ask for a grin from ear to ear,

But now no man would want you, we still do,
So cut the sulky pout. To many another
Far worse than this has happened. Ask your mother.
I don't know what the world is coming to.

See how she slinks inside. If not with grace
She seems to have accepted, more or less,
Some limit to a woman's wilfulness.
The lesson hurt us both, but met the case.

Salute me! I have tamed my daughter's face.

Stolen Children

From where I sit for cool drinks in the heat
The Covent Garden Jumpzone seems to fling
Kids over rooftops in a bungee dive
The wrong way, and the thrill it is to swing
Straight up and down you see when they arrive,
In Heaven as on Earth, with kicking feet,

And so depart. One flier takes the pip
By somersaulting in her harness when,
High overhead, there is a moment's pause
For rubber to recuperate. Not then,
But later, as she signals for applause
With a slow stride instead of a last flip,

The penny drops. I've seen this girl before.
Above the birthplace of the Son of God
It had pleased Botticelli to impose
The perfect circle of a trained cheer-squad
Dancing barefoot with light fantastic toes
As angels do, the cloudless blue their floor.

The second from the left was my dream girl.
Outside, Trafalgar Square filled up with snow.
Winter in England was a culture shock
More ways than one. The gallery's warm glow
Seemed concentrated in a flowing frock,
A flash of ankle gleaming like a pearl.

Back down with us, she saunters past my chair.
About thirteen, with more than blips for breasts,
She wasn't born before I saw her first
On a glass board surfing the troughs and crests
Of the air waves. Nor was her mother. Worst
Of all is how the longing lingers there

Yet leaves us nothing else to bless at last
Except our luck that we were not insane.
The *Standard* says the missing girls are still
Not found. A man is held. The writers strain
The law's pale letter, closing for the kill
As once the mob did, not far in the past.

Suppose he did it, don't I know that face?
I shave it every morning. The same eyes
Plead innocent. In his case, one loose screw
Switched the desire a priest can't neutralise
To children, and permitted him to do
What we don't dream of even when God's grace

Stuns us with glory walking in the sky.
Grace, but not justice. If an impulse makes
Mere fools of most but monsters of the rest,
A balance sheet of what it gives and takes
Implies a mediator who knows best
If you can just surrender. Nor can I.

Think of the fathers, praying. They must know
No-one exists to listen who did not
Choose them for this, but where else can they ask
The same exemption all the others got
By chance? They beg for mercy from a mask.
Had it a mind, they'd not be weeping so.

Time to go home. The things I tried to tell
My own two daughters churn in my hot head.
The stranger won't come on like Captain Hook.
He'll laugh like me, crack jokes, yet want you dead.
Good story, Dad. I turn for one last look
At Paradise, and how we rose and fell.

In Town for the March

Today in Castlereagh Street I
Felt short of breath, and here is why.
From the direction of the Quay
Towards where Mark Foy's used to be,
A glass and metal river ran
Made in Germany and Japan.
Past the façade of David Jones
Men walked their mobile telephones,
Making the footpath hideous
With what they needed to discuss.
But why so long, and why so loud?
I can recall a bigger crowd
In which nobody fought for space
Except to call a name. The face
To fit it smiled as it went by
Among the ranks. Women would cry
Who knew that should they call all day
One face would never look their way.
All this was sixty years ago,
Since when I have grown old and slow,
But still I see the marching men,
So many of them still young then,
Even the men from the first war
Straight as a piece of two-by-four.
Men of the Anzac Day parade,
I grew up in the world you made.
To mock it would be my mistake.
I try to love it for your sake.
Through cars and buses, on they come,
Their pace set by a spectral drum.

Their regimental banners, thin
As watercolours fading in
The sun, hint at a panoply
Dissolving into history.
As the rearguard outflanks Hyde Park,
Wheels right, and melts into the dark,
It leaves me, barely fit to stand,
Reaching up for my mother's hand.

Six Degrees of Separation from Shelley

In the last year of her life I dined with Diana Cooper
Who told me she thought the best thing to do with the poor
Was to kill them. I think her tongue was in her cheek
But with that much plastic surgery it was hard to tell.

As a child she had sat on the knee of George Meredith,
More than forty years after he published *Modern Love*.
Though she must have been as pretty as any poppet
Who challenged the trousers of Dowson or Lewis Carroll,

We can bet Meredith wasn't as modern as that.
By then the old boy wouldn't have felt a twinge
Even had he foreseen she would one day arrive
In Paris with an escort of two dozen Spitfires.

The book lamented his marriage to one of the daughters
Of Peacock. Peacock when young rescued Shelley
From a coma brought on through an excess of vegetarianism
By waving a steak under his sensitive nose.

Shelley never quite said that the best thing to do with the rich
Was to kill them, but he probably thought so.
Whether the steak was cooked or raw I can't remember.
I should, of course. I was practically there:

The blaze of his funeral pyre on the beach at night
Was still in her eyes. At her age I hope to recall
The phial of poison she carried but never used
Against the day there was nothing left to live for.

Occupation: Housewife

Advertisements asked 'Which twin has the Toni?'
Our mothers were supposed to be non-plussed.
Dense paragraphs of technical baloney
Explained the close resemblance of the phoney
To the Expensive Perm. It worked on trust.

The barber tried to tell me the same sheila
With the same Expensive Perm was pictured twice.
He said the Toni treatment was paint-sealer
Re-bottled by a second-hand car dealer
And did to hair what strychnine did to mice.

Our mothers all survived, but not the perms.
Two hours at most the Toni bobbed and dazzled
Before the waves were back on level terms,
Limp as the spear-points of the household germs
An avalanche of Vim left looking frazzled.

Another false economy, home brew
Seethed after nightfall in the laundry copper.
Bought on the sly, the hops were left to stew
Into a mulch that grunted as it grew.
You had to sample it with an eye-dropper,

Not stir it with a stick as one mum did.
She piled housebricks on top, thinking the gas
Would have nowhere to go. Lucky she hid
Inside the house. The copper blew its lid
Like Krakatoa to emit a mass

Of foam. The laundry window bulged and broke.
The prodigy invaded the back yard.
Spreading across the lawn like evil smoke
It murdered her hydrangeas at a stroke
And long before the dawn it had set hard.

On a world scale, one hardly needs to note,
Those Aussie battlers barely had a taste
Of deprivation. Reeling from the boat
Came reffo women who had eaten goat
Only on feast days. Still, it is the waste

I think of, the long years without our men,
And only the Yanks to offer luxuries
At a price no decent woman thought of then
As one she could afford, waiting for when
The Man Himself came back from Overseas.

And then I think of those whose men did not:
My mother one of them. She who had kept
Herself for him for so long, and for what?
To creep, when I had splinters, to my cot
With tweezers and a needle while I slept?

Now comes the time I fly to sit with her
Where she lies waiting, to what end we know.
We trade our stories of the way things were,
The home brew and the perm like rabbit fur.
How sad, she says, the heart is last to go.

The heart, the heart. I still can hear it break.
She asked for nothing except his return.
To pay so great a debt, what does it take?
My books, degrees, the money that I make?
Proud of a son who never seems to learn,

She can't forget I lost my good pen-knife.
Those memories of waste do not grow dim
When you, for Occupation, write: Housewife.
Out of this world, God grant them both the life
She gave me and I had instead of him.

Jesus in Nigeria

Let him so keen for casting the first stone
Direct a fast ball right between her eyes,
So it might be from one quick burst of bone,
Not from a mass of bruises, that she dies.

I'm pleased to see, of all you without sin,
The cocky dimwit is so young and strong
Who won the draw to let the games begin.
He looks the type, unless I'm very wrong,

Who'll hog the glory with his opening shot.
With any luck at least he'll knock her out.
His rivals in this miserable lot
Are hard pressed to jump up and down and shout.

That old one there has just put out his back
Lifting a boulder he could barely throw
For half a yard without a heart attack,
But you can bet, just to be in the show,

He'd shuffle up and drop it on her head.
I hate to take my father's name in vain
But God almighty, how they want her dead:
How sure they are that she should die in pain.

The woman taken in adultery:
It's one of the best stories in my book.
Some scholars call it the essential me.
If my writ ran here, you could take a look.

Alas, it doesn't. I wield little power
Even with my bunch, let alone with yours.
Long, long ago I had my public hour.
My mission failed. The maniacs and bores

Took over. I still weep, but weep in fear
Over a world become so pitiless
I miss that blessed soldier with the spear
Who put an early end to my distress.

Merely a thug and not a mental case,
He showed the only mercy I recall.
A dumb but reasonably decent face:
The best that we can hope for, all in all.

Step up, young man. Take aim and don't think twice.
No matter what you both believe is true,
Tonight she will be with me in Paradise.
I'm sorry I can't say the same for you.

The Place of Reeds

Kogarah (suppress the first 'a' and it scans)
Named by the locals for the creek's tall reeds
That look like an exotic dancer's fans
When dead, was where I lived. Born to great deeds

I stripped the fronds and was a warrior
Whose arrows were the long thin brittle stem
With a stiff piece of copper wire or
A headless nail to make a point for them.

The point went in where once the pith had been
Before it crumbled. The capillary
Was open at the other end. Some keen
Constructors mastered the technology

For fitting in a feathery tail-piece,
But they made model aeroplanes that flew.
Mine didn't, and my shafts, upon release
Wobbled and drifted as all missiles do

With nothing at the back to guide their flight.
Still, I was dangerous. My willow bow
Armed an Odysseus equipped to smite
Penelope and let her suitors go.

The creek led through a swamp where each weekend
Among the tangled trees we waged mock war.
At short range I could sometimes miss a friend
And hit the foe. Imagine Agincourt

Plus spiders, snakes and hydroponic plants.
I can't forget one boy, caught up a tree
By twenty others, peeing his short pants
As the arrows came up sizzling. It was me.

Just so the tribesmen, when our ship came in
Bringing the puffs of smoke that threw a spear
Too quick to see, realised they couldn't win.
It was our weaponry and not their fear

Defeated them. As we who couldn't lose
Fought with our toys, their young men dived for coins
From the wharf across the bay at La Perouse,
Far from us. Now, in age, my memory joins

Easy supremacy to black despair
In those enchanted gardens that they left
Because they knew they didn't have a prayer:
Lately I too begin to feel bereft.

Led by the head, my arrow proves to be
My life. I took my life into my hands.
I loosed it to its wandering apogee,
And now it falls. I wonder where it lands.

Hard-Core Orthography

In porno-speak, reversion to the Latin
Consoles us. 'Cum.' *Cum laude* we construe
As an audible orgasm. By that pattern,
Cum grano salis overturns the salt
With a thrashing climax when her urge to screw
Right there at dinner must be satisfied.
Cum vulpibus vulpinandum. While with foxes –
Caught *in flagrante*, high-heeled shoes flung wide
In satin sheets – do as the foxes do.
With aching wrist and pouting like a dolt,
Linguistically we still tick the right boxes:
You made *mecum*, she moans as she comes to.
Thus moved, her airbag lips look cumbersome
In the best sense. Maybe she's not so dumb.
Dum spiro, spero. How was it for you?

Ramifications of Pure Beauty

Passing the line-up of the narrow-boats
The swans proceed down river. As they go
They sometimes dip and lift an inch or so.
A swan is not a stick that merely floats
With the current. Currents might prove too slow
Or contrary. Therefore the feet deploy:
Trailed in the glide, they dig deep for the thrust
That makes the body bob. Though we don't see
The leg swing forward and extend, it must
Do so. Such a deduction can't destroy
Our sense-impression of serenity,
But does taint what we feel with what we know.

Bounced from up-sun by Focke-Wulf 'Long Nose'
Ta-152s, Pierre Clostermann
Noted their bodies 'fined down by the speed':
And so they were, to his eyes. Glider wings,
Long legs and close-cowled engine made the pose
Of that plane poised when stock-still. In the air,
High up and flat out, it looked fleet indeed.
What pulled it through the sky was left implied:
You had to know the turning blades were there,
Like the guns, the ammo and the man inside
Who might have thought your Tempest pretty too –
But not enough to stop him killing you.

The crowds for Titian cope with the appeal
Of flayed Actaeon. Horror made sublime:
We see that. Having seen it, we relax
With supine ladies. Pin-ups of their time,
Surely they have no hinterland of crime?
Corruption would show up like needle-tracks.
No, they are clean, as he was. All he knew
Of sin was painting them with not much on.
Even to fill a Spanish contract, he
Fleshed out the abstract with the sumptuous real –
Brought on the girls and called it poetry.
Philip II felt the same. Why think
At this late date about the mortal stink
Of the war galley, graceful as a swan?

Young Lady in Black

The Russian poets dreamed, but dreamed too soon,
Of a red-lipped, chalk-white face framed in black fur:
Symbol of what their future would be like –
Free, lyrical and elegant, like her.
In the love songs of their climacteric
I met you before I met you, and you were
The way you are now in these photographs

Your father took outside the Hermitage.
You stand on snow, and more snow in the air
Arrives in powdered form like rice through space.
It hurts to know the colour of your hair
Is blacker than your hat. Such is the price
Figments exact by turning real: we care
Too much. I too was tricked by history,

But at least I saw you, close enough to touch,
Even as time made touch impossible.
The poets never met their richly dressed
Princess of liberty. The actual girl
Was lost to them as all the rest was lost:
Only their ghosts attended the snowfall
The camera stopped when you stood in the square,

Fiction made fact at long last and too late.
My grief would look like nothing in their eyes.
I hear them in the photographs. The breath
Of sorrow stirs the cold dust while hope dies
The worst way, in the vision of rebirth,
As by whole generations they arise
From pitted shallows in the permafrost

And storm the Winter Palace from the sky.
Each spirit shivering in a bead of light,
They fall again for what they once foretold –
For you, dawn burning through its cloak of night.
They miss what I miss, and a millionfold.
It all came true, it's there in black and white:
But your mouth is the colour of their blood.

Flashback on Fast Forward

The way his broken spirit almost healed
When he first saw how lovely she could look,
Her face illuminated by a book,
Was such a holy moment that he kneeled
Beside her; and the way his shoulders shook
Moved her caressing hand. Their love was sealed.

They met again. A different, older place
Had drawn her to its books, but still the glow
Of white between the words lit up her face
As if she gazed on freshly fallen snow.
He knew his troubled heart could not forego,
Not even for her sake, this touch of grace.

He asked her hand in marriage. She said yes.
Later he often said she must have known
To be with him was to be left alone
With the sworn enemy of happiness,
Her house a demilitarised zone
At best, and peace a pause in the distress.

When finally it broke her, he helped bring
Her back to life. Give him that much at least:
His cruelty was but a casual thing,
Not a career. Alas, that thought increased
His guilt he'd talked her into sheltering
Him safe home from the storm that never ceased,

Nor ever would. And so the years went by,
And, longer wed than almost all their friends,
Always in silence they would wonder why,
And sometimes say so. When a marriage ends,
They noticed, it's from good will running dry,
Not just from lack of means to make amends.

He could not save himself: that much she knew.
Perhaps she'd felt it forty years before
When he quaked where he knelt, and what was more
She was aware that saying 'I love you'
To one who hates himself can only store
Up trouble earthly powers can't undo.

But revelation can. There at the start,
It came again to mark their closing years.
Once more, and this time through and through, his heart
Was touched. The ice he half-prized turned to tears
As the last hail-stone melts and disappears
In rain. By just a glass door set apart,

She in her study, he in the garden, they
Looked separate still, but he saw, in her eyes,
The light of the white paper. How time flies
Revealed its secret path from their first day.
He did a dance to make her look his way.
She smiled at him, her devil in disguise,

Almost as if at last he had grown wise.

The Great Wrasse: for Les Murray at sixty

Mask wet and snorkel dry, I'm lying loose
On the glass roof of time, and forty years
Straight down I see it teeming, the bombora
Of Manning House. Tables like staghorn coral
Chewed at by schools of poets. Frensham girls
(Remember Xanthe Small and Joanne Williamson,
Those blouses and tight skirts? *You little beaut*
We breathed into our fried rice. God, what dreams:
By now they must be grandmothers) glide by
Like semicircle angelfish. Psychologists
With teeth like wahoos turn their heads as one,
Torn from discussion of the Individual,
Their Watch Committee late-lunch seminar
Prorogued *pro tem.*
                          Poised Andersonian squid
Explain to freshettes peeping from their shells
If dualism allows no real division
There can be no real connection. Fusiliers,
Trevallies, sweetlips, damselfish, hussars
Patrol in Balbos, split up, feed, re-form,
Waved at by worshipping anemones.
The food chain and the mating dance, the mass
Manoeuvring, the shape-up and the shake-out,
The pretty faces pumping pain through spines:
It's all there, displayed in liquid crystal,
No further than my fingertips adrift
(A year in time is just an inch in space) –
And there *you* are, and I can see you now
For what you were, most brilliant of the bunch,
The Great Wrasse.

But to know that, I had first
To see the thing itself, in all its glory,
Five years ago. Sleeping on Lizard Island,
My family was recovering its strength
From too long in the cold. On the second day
We woke at noon and rolled into the water
To join the turtles feeding on the seagrass
Between the beach and sandbar. Serious fish
Were just around the point, at the big bommie.
We drifted off the platform at the back
Of the launch and let the current take us over
A chunk of reef that came up to arm's length:
Just what the doctor ordered. We could see
The whole aquarium in action, hear
The parrotfish at work on the hard coral
Like journalists around the Doric porch
Of some beer-froth tycoon whose time had come
To be cast out of Toorak.
                          Then it was there –
Beside us, as if to share our view:
Materialising, as is its marvellous way,
With no preliminary fanfare,
Like an air-dropped marching band that opens up
Full blast around your bed. *Lord, I can see,*
I said in silence, smiling around my rubber
Dummy like a baby. Powered by pearls
On fire inside its emerald envelope,
The Wrasse comes on like a space invader
In docking mode, filling the vision full:
The shock of its appearance stops the swimmer
Dead in the water, flippers frozen solid,
Stunned by a sudden nearness so aloof.
As if the Inca, walking his lion's walk

In soft shoes, were to pass by from behind
Preoccupied by his divinity,
So with this big fish and its quiet storm,
Its mute Magnificat.
                                    Bigger fish yet
Plumb deep holes of the Outer Barrier —
Potato cod in mottled camouflage
Like Japanese Army Kawasaki fighters
Parked in the palms, *franc-tireur* Tiger sharks
With Kerry Packer smiles, the last few marlin
To keep their swords — but nothing quite as massive
As the daddy of all wrasses, the Daimyo number,
Shows up at the bombora, and nothing as bright
Is known the whole reef over.
                                    Over the reef,
You realise, is where this fish belongs —
Above it and not of it. Nothing is written there,
Enjoyed or cherished. Even the beautiful,
There in abundance, does not know itself.
'Sex is a Nazi' you once wrote, and so
It is here. Killing to grow up so they can screw,
Things eat, are eaten, and the crown-of-thorns
Starfish that eats everything looks like
A rail map of the Final Solution,
But all it adds to universal horror
Is its lack of colour.
                                    Even in full bloom
The reef is a *jardin des supplices*:
The frills, the fronds, the fans, the powder puffs
Soften the razor's edge, the reign of terror.
Lulled by the moon snail and the Spanish dancer
With choreography by Carlos Saura,
By feathery platoons of *poules de luxe*

Cute as the kick-line of the Tropicana,
The tourist feels this is the show for him –
Atlantis in an atrium, a rumpus room
For slo-mo willy-willies of loose chips
From bombed casinos, a warehouse arcade
For love seats, swansdown pouffes and stuffed banquettes
That he could snuggle up to like a prayer
Of Hasidim against the Wailing Wall
And soothe his fevered brow in yielding plush –
But only an expert should ever touch it
Even with rubber gloves.

                  Buyer beware,
The forms of death are not just for each other
But for us too, and not all are as ugly
As the stonefish, toadfish, puffer and striped Toby
In his leather jacket. Even a child can see
That these are kitted out for bio war:
They pull the face of neurotoxic venom.
But the cone shells that beg to be picked up
By writers are like antique fountain pens
Proust might have held except he would have written
A short book, and that dreamboat with the sulk
Like Michelle Pfeiffer lolling in the glass
Elevator in *Scarface* is a breed
Of butterfly whose class would set you raving
At closer quarters, anguish cloaked in floating
Come-hither chiffon veils that spell curtains
At the first kiss.

            Rising above it all,
A benign airship poised over New York –
The *Hindenburg* without the *Hakenkreuz*
Or parking problems – just by its repose
The dawdling Wrasse siphons up Hell's Kitchen

And turns it to serenity, the spectrum
Of helium in Rutherford's radon tube,
The clear, blue light of pure polonium,
The green, fused sand of Trinity, the silent
Summary, the peaceful aftermath.
Something, someone, must be the focal emblem,
The stately bearer of the synthesis
To make our griefs make sense, if not worthwhile.
That the young you, in a red-striped sloppy joe
Like Sidney Greenstreet cast as Ginger Meggs
Progressing through the Quad the very year
Of the first Opera House Lottery draw,
Would be the Great Wrasse, few could guess
But now all know, glad that the time it took
Was in their lives, and what you made of it –
Those new and strange and lovely living things,
Your poems – theirs to goggle at when born:
Born from your mouth.
                              Born fit to breathe our sea,
Which is the air I surface to drink in
(My mask a nifty hat by Schiaparelli)
Having seen wonders – how our lives once were,
Nature's indifference, time's transparency,
Fame's cloud of pigment, fortune's blood-tipped needles,
And finally, most fabulous of all,
A monumental fish that speaks in colours,
Offering solace from within itself.

Status Quo Vadis

As any good poem is always ending,
The fence looks best when it first needs mending.
Weathered, it hints it will fall to pieces –
One day, not yet, but the chance increases
With each nail rusting and grey plank bending.
It's not a wonder if it never ceases.

In beauty's bloom you can see time burning:
A lesson learned while your guts are churning.
Her soft, sweet cheek shows the clear blood flowing
Towards the day when her looks are going
Solely to prove there is no returning
The way they came. There's a trade wind blowing.

We know all this yet we love forever.
Build her a fence and she'll think you're clever.
Write her a poem that's just beginning
From start to finish. You'll wind up winning
Her heart, perhaps, but be sure you'll never
Hold on to the rainbow the top sets spinning.

What top? The tin one that starts to shiver
Already, and soon will clatter. The river
Of colour dries up and your mother's calling
Your name while the ball hasn't finished falling,
And you miss the catch and you don't forgive her.
You went out smiling but you go home bawling.

Weep all you like. Earn your bread from weeping.
Write reams explaining there is no keeping
The toys on loan, and proclaim their seeming
Eternal glory is just the dreaming
We do pretending that we aren't sleeping –
Your tears are stinging? They're diamonds gleaming.

Think of it that way and reap the splendour
That flares reflected in the chromium fender
Of the Chrysler parked in the concrete crescent.
The surge is endless, the sigh incessant.
A revelation can only tender
Sincere regrets from the evanescent.

Remember this when it floods your senses
With streams of light and the glare condenses
Into a star. It's a star that chills you.
Don't fool yourself that the blaze fulfils you
And builds your bridges and mends your fences
Merely because of the way it thrills you –

The breath of life is what finally kills you.

Special Needs

In the clear light of a cloudy summer morning
The idiot boy, holding his father's hand,
Comes by me on the Quay where I sit writing.
His father spots me looking up, and I don't want
To look as if I wished I hadn't, so
Instead of turning straight back to my books
I look around, thus making it a general thing
That I do every so often –
To watch the ferries, to check out the crowd.
The father's eyes try not to say 'Two seconds
Is what you've had of looking at my boy.
Try half a lifetime.' Yes, the boy is bad:
So bad he holds one arm up while he walks
As if to ward off further blows from heaven.
His face reflects the pain at work behind it,
But he can't tell us what it is:
He can only moan its secret name.
The Nazis, like the Spartans, would have killed him,
But where are the Spartans and the Nazis now?
And really a sense of duty set in early,
Or at least a sense of how God's ways were strange:
After the death of Alexander
The idiot boy Philip was co-regent
To the throne of a whole empire,
And lasted in the role for quite a while
Before his inevitable murder,
Which he earned because of somebody's ambition,
And not because he couldn't clean his room.
They're gone. I can look down again, two thoughts
Contesting in my head:

'It's so unfair, I don't know what to do'
Is one. The other is the one that hurts:
'Don't be a fool. It's nothing to do with you.'
A lady wants a book signed.
I add 'Best wishes' –
All I will do today of being kind –
And when I hand it back to her, the sun
Comes out behind her. I hold up one arm.

Double or Quits

Sydney, 2006

Only when we are under different skies
The truth strikes home of what love has become:
A compact it takes time to realise
Is better far, being less burdensome,
Than that first tempest by which we were torn.
Tonight you're there, where both of us now live,
And I am here, where both of us were born,
But there is no division we need give
A thought to, beyond localised regret:
For we will be together again soon,
And both see the one sunrise and sunset
And the face saved and the face lost by the moon –
The clouds permitting, which they seldom do
In England, but at least I'll be with you.

I'll be with you from now on to the end
If you say so. Should you choose otherwise
Then I will be a jealous loving friend
To wish you well yet prove it never dies,
Desire. Your beauty still bewilders me
Though half a century has passed. I still
Stand breathless at the grace of what I see:
More so than ever, now the dead leaves fill
The garden. A long distance will soon come.
Today, no. Nor tomorrow. But it must
Open the door into Elysium
For one of us, and me the first, I trust.
May we stay joined, as these two sonnets are –
That meet, and are apart, but just so far.

Natural Selection

The gradual but inexorable magic
That turned the dinosaurs into the birds
Had no overt, only a hidden, logic.
To start the squadrons climbing from the herds
No wand was ever waved, but afterwards
Those who believed there must have been a wizard
Said the whole show looked too well-planned for hazard.

And so it does, in retrospect. Such clever
Transitions, intricate beyond belief!
The little lobsters, in their mating fever,
Assaulted from the sea, stormed up the cliff,
And swept inland as scorpions. But if
Some weapons freak equipped their tails for murder
He must have thought sheer anguish all in order.

Source of all good and hence of evil, pleasure
And hence of pain, he is, or else they are,
Without a moral sense that we can measure,
And thus without a mind. Better by far
To stand in awe of blind chance than to fear
A conscious mechanism of mutation
Bringing its fine intentions to fruition

Without a qualm about collateral horror.
The peacock and the tapeworm both make sense.
Nobody calls the ugly one an error.
But when a child is born to pain intense
Enough to drive its family all at once
To weep blood, an intelligent designer
Looks like a torture garden's beaming owner.

No, give it up. The world demands our wonder
Solely because no feeling brain conceived
The thumb that holds the bamboo for the panda.
Creation, if the thing's to be believed –
And only through belief can life be loved –
Must do without that helping hand from Heaven.
Forget it, lest it never be forgiven.

Dreams before Sleeping

The idea is to set the mind adrift
And sleep comes. Mozart, exquisitely dressed,
Walks carefully to work between soft piles
Of fresh horse-dung. Nice work. Why was my gift –
It's sixty years now and I'm still obsessed –
Hidden behind the tree? I cried for miles.
No one could find it. Find the tiger's face.
It's in the tree: i.e. the strangest place.

But gifts were presents then. In fact, for short,
We called them pressies, which was just as long,
But sounded better. Mallarmé thought 'night'
A stronger word than *nuit*. Nice word. The fort
Defied the tide but faded like a song
When the wave's edge embraced it at last light.
Which song? Time, time, it is the strangest thing.
The Waves. The Sea, the Sea. Awake and Sing.

Wrong emphasis, for music leads to sex.
Your young man must be stroking you awake
Somewhere about now, in another time.
Strange thing. Range Rover. Ducks de Luxe. *Lex rex.*
The cherry blossoms fall into the lake.
The carp cruise undisturbed. Lemon and lime
And bitters is a drink for drinkers. Just.
I who was iron burn in silence. Rust.

What would you do to please me, were you here?
The *tarte tatin* is melting the ice cream.
One sip would murder sleep, but so does this.
Left to itself, the raft floats nowhere near

Oblivion, or even a real dream.
Strange word, nice question. Real? Real as a kiss,
Which never lasts, but proves we didn't waste
The time we spent in longing for its taste.

Seek sleep and lose it. Fight it and it comes.
I knew that, but it's too late now. The bird
Sings with its wings. The turtle storms ashore.
Pigs fly. Would that translate to talking drums?
Nice if they didn't understand a word
Each other said, but drowned in metaphor –
As we do when we search within, and find
Mere traces of the peace we had in mind.

Forget about it. Just get up and write.
But when you try to catch that cavalcade,
Too much coherence muscles in. Nice thought.
Let's hear it, heartbreak. Happiness writes white.
Be grateful for the bed of nails you made
And now must lie in, trading, as you ought,
Sleep for the pictures that will leave you keen
To draft a memo about what they mean.

You will grow weary doing so. Your eyes
Are fighting to stay open. When they fail
You barely make it back to where you lay.
What do you see? Little to memorize.
A lawn shines green again through melting hail.
Deep in its tree, a tiger turns away.
Nice try, but it was doomed, that strange request
To gaze into the furnace and find rest.

Naomi from Namibia

In the Brisbane Botanical Gardens,
Walking the avenue of weeping figs,
You can see exuded latex stain the bark
Like adolescent sperm. A metamorphosis:
The trunks must be full of randy boys.

At home, the Java willows
When planted alongside a watercourse
Were said to stem the breeding of mosquitoes.
Here, they have nothing else to do
Except to stand there looking elegant
In Elle McPherson lingerie.

From the walkway through the mangrove mud-flats
Spread south from overwhelming Asia,
You can see the breathing tubes of Viet Cong crabs
And imagine Arnie hiding from the Predator
Like a mud-skipper playing possum,
Although he did that, of course, in South America.
Below the tangled branches, bubbles tick.

For a century and a half, the giant banyan
Has grown like a cathedral heading downwards,
As a dumb Chartres might slowly dive for cover
Through shallows clear as air. In India
At least a dozen families would be dying
By inches in its colonnades.

At the kiosk, Naomi from Namibia
Serves me a skimmed milk strawberry milkshake.
She has come here to lead her ideal life,
Like almost all these trees.
They get to stay, but she has to go back.

Fires Burning, Fires Burning

Over Hamburg in March 1943
The Lancaster crews could feel the heat
Through the sides of the aircraft.
The fire was six thousand feet high.

Further East, there were other fires.
When burning a lot of bodies, the SS found
The thing to do was to put down a layer
Of women first.
They had more fat in them.

In Tokyo, on the night of March 9th 1945,
Some people who survived in a canal
Saw a horse on fire running through the streets.
But few who saw it were left to remember anything:
Even the water burned.

In New York, on September 11th 2001,
Some couples, given the choice
Between the flames and a long fall,
Outflanked the heat and went down holding hands.
Come with me, you imagine the men saying,
I know a quicker way.

Sydney, two years later. Next to my mother's coffin
I gave thanks that she would shortly meet
A different kind of fire,
Having died first, and in due time.

Return of the Lost City

How far was Plato free of that 'inflamed
Community' he said we should avoid?
Sofas, incense and hookers: these he named
Among the habits not to be enjoyed,
And if you did, you ought to be ashamed.
But can't we tell, by how he sounds annoyed,
That his Republic, planned on our behalf,
Was where his own desires had the last laugh,

If only as the motor for his sense
Of discipline? Even the dreams were policed,
By the Nocturnal Council. Such immense
Powers of repression! What would be released
Without them? The Republic was intense:
The fear of relaxation never ceased.
Hence the embargo on all works of art,
However strict in form, that touched the heart.

No poetry. No poets! No, not one –
Not even Homer, if he were to be
Reborn – could be admitted, lest the sun
Set on the hard-won social harmony,
And that obscene night-life which had begun
In man's first effort at society,
Atlantis, should come flooding back, the way
The sea did, or so story-tellers say.

But Plato knew that they'd say anything:
For money or applause or just a share
Of an hetaera, they would dance and sing
And turn the whole deal into a nightmare.

The very prospect left him quivering
With anger. There is something like despair
Haunting the author of the ideal state,
A taunting voice he heard while working late:

Atlantis made you. It is what you know,
Deep down. Atlantis and its pleasures drive
Your thoughts. Atlantis never lets you go.
Atlantis is where you are most alive –
Yes, even you, you that despise it so,
When all mankind would love it to arrive
Again, the living dream you try to kill
By making perfect. But you never will.

Museum of the Unmoving Image

The objects on display might seem to lack
Significance, unless you know the words.
The final straw that broke the camel's back,
The solitary stone that killed two birds.

Does this stuff really merit a glass case?
A tatty mattress and a shrivelled pea,
A shadow that somebody tried to chase,
A rusty pin that somehow earned a fee?

That gilded lily might have looked quite good
Without the dust that you won't see me for.
But where's the thrill in one piece of touched wood?
I think we've seen that uncut ice before.

A strained-at gnat, how interesting is that?
The bat from hell looks pitifully tame,
As do the pickled tongue got by the cat,
The ashes of the moth drawn to the flame.

Spilled milk, rough diamond, gift horse, gathered moss,
Dead duck, gone goose, bad apple, busted flush –
They're all lined up as if we gave a toss.
Try not to kill each other in the crush.

They've got an annexe for the big events:
Burned boats and bridges, castles in the air,
Clouds for your head to be in, rows of tents
For being camp as. Do we have to care?

What does this junk add up to? Look and learn,
The headphones say. They say our language grew
Out of this bric-a-brac. Here we return
To when the world around us shone brand new,

Lending its lustre to what people said;
Their speech was vivid with specific things.
It cries out to be brought back from the dead.
See what it was, and hear what it still sings.

A Gyre from Brother Jack

The canvas, called *A Morning Long Ago*,
Hangs now in Dublin's National Gallery
Of Ireland, and for capturing the flow
Of life, its radiant circularity,
Yeats painter leaves Yeats poet beaten flat.
I hear you saying, 'How can he say that?'

But look. Here is the foyer of a grand
Theatre. It is always interval.
On the upper level, brilliant people stand.
What they have seen inside invests them all
With liquid light, and some of them descend
The sweet, slow, curving, anti-clockwise bend

Of staircase and go out into that park
Where yet another spectacle has formed:
A lake made bright by the oncoming dark.
And at the left of that, white wings have stormed
Upward towards where this rondeau begins.
Birds? Angels? Avatars? Forgiven sins?

He doesn't say: the aspect I like best.
William had theories. Jack has just the thrill.
We see a little but we miss the rest,
And what we keep to ponder, time will kill.
The lives we might have led had we but known
Check out at dawn and take off on their own

Even as we arrive. Sad, it might seem,
When talked about: but shown, it shines like day.
The only realistic general scheme
Of the divine is in this rich display –
Proof that the evanescent present tense
Is made eternal by our transience.

Diamond Pens of the Bus Vandals

Where do bus vandals get their diamond pens
That fill each upstairs window with a cloud
Of shuffled etchings? Patience does them proud.
Think of Spinoza when he ground a lens.

A fog in London used to be outside
The bus, which had to crawl until it cleared.
Now it's as if the world had disappeared
In shining smoke however far you ride.

You could call this a breakthrough, of a sort.
These storms of brilliance, light as the new dark,
Disturb and question like a pickled shark:
Conceptual art free from the bonds of thought,

Raw talent rampant. New York subway cars
Once left poor Jackson Pollock looking tame.
Some of the doodlers sprayed their way to fame:
A dazzled Norman Mailer called them stars.

And wasn't Michelangelo, deep down,
Compelled to sling paint by an empty space,
Some ceiling he could thoroughly deface?
The same for Raphael. When those boys hit town

Few of its walls were safe. One cave in France
Has borne for almost forty thousand years
Pictures of bison and small men with spears –
Blank surfaces have never stood a chance

Against the human impulse to express
The self. All those initials on the glass
Remind you, as you clutch your Freedom Pass,
It's a long journey from the wilderness.

When We Were Kids

When we were kids we fought in the mock battle
With Ned Kelly cap guns and we opened the cold bottle
Of Shelley's lemonade with a Scout belt buckle.
We cracked the passion fruit and sipped the honeysuckle.

When we were kids we lit the Thundercracker
Under the fruit tin and we sucked the all day sucker.
We opened the shoe box to watch the silk-worms spinning
Cocoons of cirrus with oriental cunning.

When we were kids we were sun-burned to a frazzle.
The beach was a griddle, you could hear us spit and sizzle.
We slept face down when our backs came out in blisters.
Teachers were famous for throwing blackboard dusters.

When we were kids we dive-bombed from the tower.
We floated in the inner tube, we bowled the rubber tyre.
From torn balloons we blew the cherry bubble.
Blowing up Frenchies could get you into trouble.

When we were kids we played at cock-a-lorum.
Gutter to gutter the boys ran harum-scarum.
The girls ran slower and their arms and legs looked funny.
You weren't supposed to drink your school milk in the dunny.

When we were kids the licorice came in cables.
We traded Hubba-Bubba bubblegum for marbles.
A new connie-agate was a flower trapped in crystal
Worth just one go with a genuine air pistol.

When we were kids we threw the cigarette cards
Against the wall and we lined the Grenadier Guards
Up on the carpet and you couldn't touch the trifle
Your Aunt Marge made to go in the church raffle.

When we were kids we hunted the cicada.
The pet cockatoo bit like a barracuda.
We were secret agents and fluent in pig Latin.
Gutsing on mulberries made our lips shine like black satin.

When we were kids we caught the Christmas beetle.
Its brittle wings were gold-green like the wattle.
Our mothers made bouquets from frangipani.
Hard to pronounce, a pink musk-stick cost a penny.

When we were kids we climbed peppercorns and willows.
We startled the stingrays when we waded in the shallows.
We mined the sand dunes in search of buried treasure,
And all this news pleased our parents beyond measure.

When we were kids the pus would wet the needle
When you dug out splinters and a piss was called a piddle.
The scabs on your knees would itch when they were ready
To be picked off your self-renewing body.

When we were kids a year would last forever.
Then we grew up and were told it was all over.
Now we are old and the memories returning
Are like the last stars that fade before the morning.

Private Prayer at Yasukuni Shrine

An *Oka* kamikaze rocket bomb
Sits in the vestibule, its rising sun
Ablaze with pride.
Names of the fallen are on CD-ROM.
The war might have been lost. The peace was won:
A resurrection after suicide.

For once I feel the urge to send my thoughts
Your way, as I suppose these people do.
I see the tide
Come in on Papua. Their troop transports,
The beach, our hospital. Over to you:
Why was one little miracle denied?

After they made our nurses wade waist deep
They picked their targets and they shot them all.
The waves ran red.
Somehow this is a memory I keep.
I hear the lost cries of the last to fall
As if I, too, had been among the dead.

Those same troops fought south to the Golden Stairs,
Where they were stopped. They starved, and finally
The last few fed
On corpses. And the victory would be theirs
If I were glad? That's what you're telling me?
It would have been in vain that your son bled?

But wasn't it? What were you thinking when
Our daughters died? You couldn't interfere,
I hear you say.
That must mean that you never can. Well, then,
At least I know now that no prayers from here
Have ever made much difference either way,

And therefore we weren't fighting you as well.
Old people here saw the *Missouri* loom
Out in the bay
And thought the end had come. They couldn't tell
That the alternative to certain doom
Would be *pachinko* and the cash to play

A game of chance, all day and every day.
In that bright shrine you really do preside.
What you have said
Comes true. The Dow is down on the Nikkei.
The royal baby takes a buggy ride.
The last war criminal will die in bed.

Sonnet after Wyatt

The final naked stalking feet have fled.
My chamber, even when the summer sun
Streams in to light my books, is dark instead:
Those shining walkers have all cut and run.
Out of the shower, not wearing very much,
Printing the air with pleasure for my eyes,
As sweet to look at as they were to touch,
They stepped like firebrands in a friendly guise,
Brighter than day. The voids they left behind
Ache at the point that most intensely felt
Their prettiness, where vision floods the mind
With the same heat that first made the heart melt.
So I, that now they flee but once they sought,
Pine for the sight and perish at the thought.

Paddington Departures

He was my age, and she my daughter's age:
Perhaps younger than that. I saw them kiss.
She turned and left him at the barrier.
He loitered there to watch her walk away
Along the platform. Keeping them both in sight,
I watched him watching her, until she turned
Again, and looked back. Then I knew for sure
They had made love last night. If otherwise,
His raised hand would have had much more to say,
And hers, too. They exchanged acknowledgement
Only of time: this time, next time. They were
Together, though apart. I saw it all.
It was early in the morning. He went home
And she went home. Why didn't he go with her?
Clearly because he couldn't. My own train
Waited to take me far into the West,
To slightly warmer weather, and the hall
Where I would read my poems about loss,
Having lost nothing since the last blue moon
To touch what I'd just seen. Alone for good
Is not the same thing as alone for now,
Nor she who won't return as she who will –
Departing only to appear again,
Filling the outline of a memory
Until the real farewell, when the tears fall,
And her not being there is always there.

Literary Lunch

Reciting poetry by those you prize –
Auden, MacNeice, Yeats, Stevens, Charlotte Mew –
I trust my memory and watch your eyes
To see if you know I am wooing you
With all these stolen goods. Of course you do.

Across the table, you know every line
Does service for a kiss or a caress.
Words taken out of other mouths, in mine
Are a laying on of hands in formal dress,
And your awareness measures my success

While marking out its limits. You may smile
For pleasure, confident my love is pure:
What would have been an exercise in guile
When I was young and strong, is now for sure
Raised safely to the plane of literature,

Where you may take it as a compliment
Unmixed with any claims to more delight
Than your attention. Such was my intent
This morning, as I planned what to recite
Just so you might remember me tonight,

When you are with the man who has no need
Of any words but his, or even those:
The only poem that he cares to read
Is open there before him. How it flows
He feels, and how it starts and ends he knows.

Exit Don Giovanni

Somewhere below his pride, the Don's bad dreams
Fashioned the statue that would take him down.
Deep underground, the tears were there in streams.
The man who had the only game in town,

In Spain, in Europe, when it came to love,
Sensed that there had to be a reckoning.
The boundaries he claimed to soar above
Meant nothing to him except everything.

Why the defiant stance, if not from shame?
And why deny that truth, if not from fear?
The bodice-ripper made his famous name
By staying buttoned up. His whole career

Came back to haunt him in a stony glance.
Transfixed, he followed where the statue led.
Below, tips of hot tongues began to dance.
Further below, it was a sea of red.

There was a jetty. Next to it, a raft
Held every name on Leporello's list,
Even from just last week. The statue laughed
And left. The women, modelled out of mist,

Were images, as they had always been
To him, but strong enough to ply the sweeps.
They would not meet his eye, having foreseen
What waited for him on the burning deeps.

A long way out, they paused, and one by one
They disappeared, each hinting with a smile,
But not to him, their work had been well done.
He was alone. To cry was not his style,

But then he reached down through the surface fire
Into the water. Almost with relief
He learned at last the flames of his desire
Had floated on the ocean of his grief.

Had he known sooner, what would that have meant?
Less to regret, and little to admit?
The raft burned: final stage of his descent.
Hell was on Earth. Now he was out of it.

Press Release from Plato

Delayed until the sacred ship got back
From Delos, the last hour of Socrates
Unfolded smoothly. His time-honoured knack
For putting everybody at their ease

Was still there even while the numbness spread
Up from his feet. All present in the cell
Were much moved by the way he kept his head
As he spoke less, but never less than well.

Poor Crito and Apollodorus wept
Like Xanthippe, but not one tear was his
From start to finish. Dignity was kept.
If that much isn't certain, nothing is.

I only wish I could have been there too.
When, later on, I wrote down every word,
I double-checked – the least that I could do –
To make it sound as if I'd overheard.

But let's face facts. He lives because of me.
That simple-seeming man and what he meant
To politics and to philosophy –
These things have not survived by accident.

Deals to be done and details to discuss
Called me elsewhere. I'm sorry for that still.
He owed a cock to Aesculapius.
Socratic question: guess who paid the bill?

You, Mark Antony

The sex, good from the start, just kept on getting
Better. She shook, she shrieked, she shouted words
In her strange language full of dogs and birds,
Sank prettily into sleep like the sun setting

Before she rose again, hungry for kissing:
And each kiss asked him back to plumb the sweet
Depth of her lilting hips and lactic heat.
'I never even knew what I was missing,'

He sighed to Enobarbus. 'When she's coming
She pulses in there like a pigeon's throat.
I swear that royal pussy sings a note.
I stuck my head down there and heard it humming.'

A foul tongue spared the general from admitting
In his own mind that what he really felt
Was passion fit to make his armour melt.
Manly obscenities were far more fitting.

The two men who once spent their evenings drinking
Now talked only at breakfast. She slept late.
Her afternoons were for affairs of state.
Her nights however, were for him. Just thinking

About her left him helpless. There's no knowing
If his lieutenant guessed ahead of time
This raging folly would lead to the crime
Of cowardice, and that the world was going

To pieces. If he did, he wasn't saying:
That Antony would brook no argument
Was plain. If nothing else was while things went
Haywire, it might be like a tooth decaying:

It might drop out, he might get well, quit fooling
Around when he had had enough of her:
When he had sucked her nectar, as it were,
So long he was ashamed to be seen drooling.

But Antony was toast. He kept returning
To the only battlefield where victory
Is measured by the victim's ecstasy,
And one soft cry is worth a city burning.

He died thinking of her, and knew when dying
She'd been the death of him. The world well lost?
It might not seem so when we count the cost,
But if we call him thoughtless we are lying

About ourselves and those long nights of stewing
In our own juice for somebody who tore
Our lives apart and whom we still adore –
And all the time we knew what we were doing.

State Funeral

in memory of Shirley Strickland de la Hunty

Famous for overcoming obstacles
She finally finds one that checks her flight.
Hit by the leading foot, a hurdle falls:
Except when, set in concrete, it sits tight.

Not that she hit too many. Most she cleared,
Her trailing leg laid effortlessly flat.
As in repose, at full tilt she appeared
Blessed with a supple grace. On top of that

She studied physics, took a good degree,
Had several languages to read and speak.
Alone, she wasn't short of company:
In company she shone. She was unique

Even among our girl Olympians
For bringing the mind's power and body's poise
To perfect balance. Ancient Greeks had plans
Along those lines, but strictly for the boys.

Her seven medals in three separate Games
Should have been eight, but she retired content.
In time she sold the lot to feed the flames
Of her concern for the Environment.

Civic responsibility: but one
Kind of pollution lay outside her scope
To counteract. The races she had run
Were won now by sad cyborgs fuelled with dope.

It started in the East. The State required
Results that only science could supply.
The female victims, suitably rewired
For victory, could do everything but fly.

And if some wept for how they changed, too bad.
The doctors did what they were ordered to
And told the chosen ones they should be glad:
Drink this, and it will make a man of you.

The plague spread to the West, where money talked.
Poor women, like poor men, had much to gain
Through muscle. The bad bottle was uncorked.
They plucked their chins and thought it worth the pain.

Perhaps it was, yet one glimpse of Flo-Jo
Coiled in her starting blocks told you the cost.
Transmuted to a charging buffalo,
She mourned with painted nails for what she'd lost.

But more was lost than that. The time had come
When no-one could be trusted any more
Because to play it straight seemed simply dumb,
And who remembered how things were before?

Desire beats scruple into second place.
Gratification makes a fool of thrift.
The only rules are Rafferty's. The race
Is to the sly that once was to the swift.

A brighter future, back there in the past,
Flared for a moment but it flickered out.
It speaks, our flag that flutters at half mast,
Of final silence. Let it silence doubt:

When Shirley raced, the wings on her spiked shoes
Were merely mythical, like Mercury's.
She did it unassisted, win or lose.
The world she did it in died by degrees

While she looked on. Now she is spared the sight
At last. The bobby-dazzler won't be back,
Who ran for love and jumped for sheer delight
In a better life and on a different track —

We have too much if she is what we lack.

Publisher's Party

for Posy Simmonds

Young ladies beautiful as novelists
Were handing out the nibbles and the drinks.
Butch writers with bald heads and hairy wrists
Exchanged raised eyebrows, nudges, knowing winks,
Hints broader than their beams.
The tall dark knockout who prowled like a lynx
With the chicken satay cooled the optimists –
Her polite smile said 'as if' and 'in your dreams'.

One writer never sought her violet eyes.
He concentrated on the parquet floor.
Ungainly yet of no impressive size,
Lacking in social skills, licensed to bore,
He was the kind of bloke
A girl like her would normally ignore,
Unless, of course, he'd won the Booker Prize.
Alas, he had. I can't think of a joke –

Only of how she lingered there until
He woke up to the full force of her looks;
Of how we rippled with a jealous thrill,
All those of us who'd also written books
Out of an inner need;
And now a panel-game of hacks and crooks
Had staked him out for her to stalk and kill –
As if the man could write, and she could read.

They live in Docklands now: a top-floor flat
They can see France from. Yes, they live there, too:
A house in the Dordogne. Stuff like that
I honestly don't care about, do you?
But then I see her face
Beside his in the papers. Strange, but true –
Blind chance that picked his fame out of a hat
Had perfect vision when it gave him grace.

My new book's hopeless and I'm getting fat.

The Zero Pilot

On the *Hiryu*, Hajime Toyoshima
Starred in the group photos like Andy Hardy,
He was so small and cute.
His face, as friendly as his first name
(In Japanese you say 'Hajime' at first meeting),
Could have been chirping, 'Hey, why don't we
Put the show on right here in the barn?'
After Pearl Harbour he was one of the great ship's heroes
And the attack on Darwin promised him yet more glory,
But his engine conked out over Melville Island
From one lousy rifle bullet in the oil system.
Caught by natives, he should have done it then,
If not beforehand when the prop stopped turning.
Instead of hitting the silk
He could have nosed over and dived into the ground
But he didn't. When the natives closed in
He could have shot himself with his .32
But he didn't do that either.
Under interrogation he was offered chocolate
Which he ate instead of turning down.
What was he thinking of?
He didn't get it done
Until a full two and half years later –
After the Cowra breakout, which he helped
To lead, madly blowing a stolen bugle,
Psyched up to guide his party of frantic runners
All the way to Japan. Upon recapture
He finally did it with a carving knife,
Sawing at his own throat as if to cancel
That sweet, rich taste of surrender,

The swallowed chocolate. His ruined Zero
Is on display in Darwin. The empty bulkhead
Is torn like silver paper where the engine roared
That once propelled him through the startled sky
At a rate of roll unknown to Kittyhawks.
Paint, cables, webbing, instruments and guns:
Much else is also missing,
But the real absence is his,
And always was.
'Hajime' is short for
'Our acquaintanceship begins:
Until now, we did not know each other.
From this day forth, we will'.
Well, could be,
Though it mightn't be quite that easy.
Buried at Cowra,
He probably never knew
That the *Hiryu* went down at Midway,
Where the last of his friends died fighting –
Still missing the cheery voice
Of their mascot, named always to say hello,
Who never said goodbye.

Iron Horse

The Sioux, believing ponies should be pintos,
Painted the ones that weren't.
When they saw the Iron Horse
They must have wondered why the palefaces
Left its black coat unmarked.
Bruno Schulz said an artist must mature
But only into childhood.
He called our first perceptions
The iron capital of the adult brain.
I would like to think my latest marquetry
Was underpinned by Debussy's *Images*
Or the chain of micro-essays
In Adorno's *Minima moralia*,
But a more likely progenitor
Entered my head right here in Sydney:
The first aesthetic thrill that I remember.
In a Strand Arcade display case
A tiny but fine-detailed model train
Ran endlessly around a plaster landscape.
On tip-toe, looking through the panorama
Rather than down on it, I formed or fed
Lasting ideals of mimesis, precision
And the consonance of closely fitted parts
Combined into a work that had coherence
Beyond its inseparable workings.
Later, at the flicks, when the Iron Horse
Was attacked by yelping braves,
I heard their hoof-beats on a marble floor,
And later still, having read about steam power
In my *Modern Marvels Encyclopaedia*,

When I realised the little train
Had been pulled by an illusionary loco –
Directly turned by an electric motor,
The wheels propelled the rods and not vice versa –
My seeing through the trick only increased
The recollection of intensity,
Immensity compressed into a bubble,
The macrosphere in miniature.
But mere shrinkage didn't work the magic:
There had to be that complicated movement
Of intricate articulation
As in an aero engine like the Merlin
Or the H-form Napier Sabre.
In the Hermitage, a Fabergé toy train
Was not so precious, didn't even go,
Was hopelessly disfigured by its jewels.
It left me with pursed lips and shaking head,
Surprised they even bothered
And full of pity for the royal children
Deceived by their bonanza every Christmas –
A wampum headband set with amethysts,
A solid silver tomahawk –
Into equating workmanship with wealth.
Full of boutiques that try to do the same,
The Strand Arcade is still there,
Commendably preserved if over-polished,
But the train is gone for good –
Except where, in my mind,
Forever turning back and yet forever
Continuing its *tour d'horizon*

Of a world threatened by a race of giants,
It snickers behind the glass
I stained with the acid of my fingertips.

Statement from the Secretary of Defense

This one we didn't know we didn't know:
At least, I didn't. You, you might have known
You didn't know. Let's say that might be so.
You knew, with wisdom granted you alone,

You didn't know. You say, but don't say how,
You knew we didn't know about abuse,
By us, in gaols of theirs that we run now.
Well, now we all know. I make no excuse:

In fact it's far worse than you think. You thought
You knew how bad it was? If you could see
The photos in this classified report
You'd know you knew, as usual, less than me.

You want to see a stress position? Look
At how I crouch to meet the President
And tell him this has not gone by the book.
How do I know he won't know what I meant?

I just know what he'll say, with hanging head:
'They don't know what pain is, these foreign folks.
Pain is to know you don't know what gets said
Behind your back, except you know the jokes.'

I feel for that man in his time of trial.
He simply didn't know, but now he knows
He didn't, and it hurts. Yet he can smile.
Remember how that Arab saying goes –

The blow that doesn't break you makes you strong?
They'll thank us when they get up off the mat.
They didn't know we knew what they knew. Wrong.
Even our women can do stuff like that.

Fair-weather friends who called our cause so good
Not even we could screw it, but now say
We've managed the impossible – I've stood
All I can stand of petty spite today,

So leave no room for doubt: now that we know
We might have known we didn't know, let's keep
Our heads. Give history time, and time will show
How flags wash clean, and eagles cease to weep.

Angels over Elsinore

How many angels knew who Hamlet was
When they were summoned by Horatio?
They probably showed up only because
The roster said it was their turn to go.

Another day, another Dane. Too bad,
But while they sang their well-rehearsed lament
They noticed his good looks. Too soon, too sad,
This welcome home for what seemed heaven sent.

Imagine having been with him down there!
But here I dream, for angels do not yearn.
They take up their positions in the air
Free from the passions of the earth they spurn.

Even their singing is done less from joy
Than duty. But was this the usual thing?
Surely they gazed on that recumbent boy,
Clearly cut out one day to be a king,

And sang him to his early rest above
With soaring pride that they should form the choir
Whose voices echoed all the cries of love,
Which, even when divine, implies desire?

But soft: an ideal world does not exist.
Hamlet went nowhere after he was dead.
No angel sighed where lovers never kissed,
And there was nothing in what his friend said.

Hamlet himself knew just what to expect:
Steady reduction of his body mass
Until the day, his very coffin wrecked,
Some clown picked up his skull and said, 'Alas.'

No, there would be no music from on high.
No feather from a wing would fall, not one.
Forget it all, even the empty sky –
What's gone is gone, sweet prince. What's done is done.

Young Lady Going to Dakar

Another annual boat trip from Le Havre
To Bordeaux, but this time different. When Lautrec
Beheld the girl from Cabin 54
On deck reading, he decided to stay on
Until Lisbon at least. Painting had raised
The Paris cabarets, dance-halls and brothels
To angelic levels, but this unclouded creature
Started where all that finished. How not dream –
As she in her deckchair read and he nearby
Sketched for *La Passagère du cinquante-quatre:*
Promenade en yacht – that she would see his tears
And ask him to come with her to Dakar,
There to return his looks with the same favour,
Even for his legs? The painter's friend
Maurice Gilbert howled down the mad idea
Of Africa. They got off at Lisbon
And returned to Bordeaux overland.
In Toledo, for the first time in his life,
He saw El Greco. Dry-eyed, he took on
More strength, as if more strength were what he needed,
And not what he would instantly have traded
For just one glance from her untouched by pity:
Not even playful. Casual would have done.
The naked flame behind that cabin door!
Perish the thought. Paint her and finish her,
Drowned like the Holy Name in molten gold.

Only Divine

Always the Gods learned more from humankind
Than vice versa. So it was bound to be:
It takes a troubled heart to make a mind.
Stuck with their beautiful stupidity,

The Gods were peeved to find themselves outclassed
Even in pleasure, which was their best thing.
Sky-walking Zeus, the Bright One, was aghast
To find that men could laugh and weep and sing

For love, instead of merely chasing tail
The way he did when he came down to earth:
Driving his lightning bolt in like a nail,
Shouting the place down with unsubtle mirth.

Sometimes he stole earth-men's identities.
His acrobatics in a borrowed face
Drew some applause for their raw power to please
But none at all for foreplay, tact or grace.

By Jove! By Jupiter! He heard the names
Men gave him change. The world grew less impressed
Than he was with his simple fun and games,
The gold medallions on his hairy chest.

Back in the clouds, he brooded for as long
As Gods can. If he couldn't have the tears
Of mortals, he could copy a love song.
To learn one took him several hundred years,

But time, like sorrow, doesn't count up there.
He got quite good at it, and now he sings
Sinatra standards that sound pretty fair
Against a backing track complete with strings.

Virgin Minerva, born out of his brain
To stave off Vulcan with a single slap,
Borrowed more fetching versions of disdain
Better designed to milk the thunderclap

Of lust. Her heavenly suitors pay for shoes
She might wear only once, or not at all.
Pretending they know how it feels to lose,
Prospective lovers, outside in the hall,

Compare TAG Heuer watches while they scuff
Their Gucci loafers on the marble floor.
In love, real men have taught them, things get rough:
A show of grief might get you through her door.

Inside, she lies back on her Zsa-Zsa pink
Chaise-longue while Aphrodite dishes dirt.
Feigning to taste the whisky sours they drink,
They smile as if a memory could hurt.

Does Atlas need those Terminator shades?
Poseidon's wet-suit, what good does it do?
Is gold-crowned Phoebe on her roller blades
Really as cute as when the world was new?

And here comes Hera in her Britney kit,
And there goes Hermes on his superbike.
The stuff they have! You wouldn't credit it,
And all top of the range. What are they *like*?

Like us, without the creativity
Stirred by the guilt that hangs around our necks.
Their only care the void of their carefree
Millennia of unprotected sex,

Uncomprehendingly they quote our books.
Their gull-wing sports cars and their Gulfstream jets,
The bling-bling wasted on their perfect looks –
It's all ours. Gleaming as their long sun sets,

The Gods are gaudy tatters of a plan
Hatched by our ancestors to render fate
More bearable. They end as they began,
Belittled in our thoughts that made them great.

My Father before Me

Sai Wan War Cemetery, Hong Kong

At noon, no shadow. I am on my knees
Once more before your number and your name.
The usual heat, the usual fretful bees
Fitfully busy as last time I came.

Here you have lain since 1945,
When you, at half the age that I am now,
Were taken from the world of the alive,
Were taken out of time. You should see how

This hillside, since I visited it first,
Has stayed the same. Nothing has happened here.
They trim the sloping lawn and slake its thirst.
Regular wreaths may fade and reappear,

But these are details. High on either side
Waves of apartment blocks roll in so far
And no further, forbidden to collide
By laws that keep the green field where you are,

Along with all these others, sacrosanct.
For once the future is denied fresh ground.
For that much if no more, let God be thanked.
You can't see me or even hear the sound

Of my voice, though it comes out like the cry
You heard from me before you sailed away.
Your wife, my mother, took her turn to die
Not long ago. I don't know what to say –

Except those many years she longed for you
Are over now at last, and now she wears
The same robes of forgetfulness you do.
When the dreams cease, so do the nightmares.

I know you would be angry if I said
I, too, crave peace. Besides, it's not quite so.
Despair will ebb when I leave you for dead
Once more. Once more, as I get up to go,

I look up to the sky, down to the sea,
And hope to see them, while I still draw breath,
The way you saw your photograph of me
The very day you flew to meet your death.

Back at the gate, I turn to face the hill,
Your headstone lost again among the rest.
I have no time to waste, much less to kill.
My life is yours, my curse to be so blessed.

The Magic Wheel

an ode in the manner of Theocritus

O magic wheel, draw hither to my house the man I love.
I dreamed of you as dreaming that, and now
The boxed-in balcony of my hotel room high above
Grand Harbour is a sauna. See the prow
Of that small boat cut silk. Out in the sea
No waves, and there below not even ripples turning light
To glitter: just a glow spread evenly
On flawless water spills into the skyline that last night
Was a jewelled silhouette from right to left and left to right.

Behold, the sea is silent, and silent are the winds.
The not yet risen sun edges the sky
With petal-juice of the Homeric rose as day begins.
I am alone, but with you till I die,
Now we have met again after six years.
Last night we danced on limestone in the open-air café.
I saw one woman sitting there near tears,
Aware that she would never look like you or dance that way –
A blessing, like the blessings that have brought you home to stay.

O magic wheel, draw hither to my house the man I love.
I dreamed of you as dreaming that, until
I saw you wave in welcome from your window high above,
And up the slick hard steps designed to kill,
Like all Valletta staircases bar none,
I went, as if I still had strength, to find your open door
And you, and your tremendous little son,

And your husband, the great dancer, whom I had not met before,
And I met his kindly eyes and knew you dreamed of me no more.

Behold, the sea is silent, and silent are the winds.
Stirred by the ceiling fan, the heat of noon
Refuses to grow cooler as it very slowly spins,
But I take its rearrangement as a boon,
As if it were the gradual work of time,
Which leaves things as they are but changes us and picks the hour
To make us see resentment is a crime.
A loving memory forgets and true regret yields power:
Trust in the long slow aqueduct and not the water tower.

O magic wheel, draw hither to my house the man I love.
I dreamed of you as dreaming that. Tonight
My dream was gone, but flowering in the darkness high above
The *festa*, rockets set the rain alight,
The soft, sweet rain. With you and your young men,
I walked the shining streets and all was right and nothing wrong
As the joy of our first moment lived again.
In the ruins of the opera house a lizard one inch long
Is the small but vibrant echo of an interrupted song.

Bethink me of my love and whence it comes, O holy Moon.
I dreamed of you as dreaming that, and now
I know you never did. Another day: the afternoon
Burns white as only here the sun knows how,
But a fever is broken when I sweat –
For my delight in your contentment proves that in the past
My love must have been true, as it is yet:
The magic wheel has turned to show what fades and what holds fast.
Dream this when I am gone: that he was glad for me at last.

The Serpent Beguiled Me

Following Eve, you look for apple cores
Along the riverbank, tossed in the mud.
Following Adam down long corridors,
You swing your torch to look for spit and blood.

He got his chest condition when he learned
Contentment made her curious. He thought
He was enough for her, and what he earned
Would keep her pinned while he played covert sport.

Alas, not so. She claimed that privilege too,
And even, under wraps, nursed the same pride
In taking satiation as her due –
A cue to call herself dissatisfied.

That rate of change was coded by the tree
Into the fruit. The instant thrill of sin
Turned sweet release to bitter urgency:
His fig leaf was flicked off, and hers sucked in.

From that day forth, the syrup she gave down
Smacked of the knowledge that she felt no shame.
The modesty for which she won renown
Was feigned to keep her freedom free of blame.

There was a time when, if he had not worn
Her out, she would have lain awake and wept.
Why was the truth, we ask, so slow to dawn?
He should have guessed it from how well she slept.

And when she turned to him, as she did still,
Though the old compulsion was no longer there,
The readiness with which she drank her fill
Told him in vain her fancy lay elsewhere.

He never faced the fact until she went.
He tracked her down and asked her what was wrong.
For once she said exactly what she meant:
'It was perfect. It just went on too long.'

Woman Resting

Sometimes the merely gifted give us proof
Born artists have a democratic eye
That genius gets above, to stand aloof,
Scorning to seize on all that happens by

And give it the full treatment. Look at her,
Mancini's woman, as she rests her head
In white impasto linen. Cats would purr
To think of lying curled up on that bed

Warmed by her Monica Bellucci skin.
Her mouth, like Vitti's in *La Notte*, breathes
A sulky need for more of the same sin
That knocked her sideways. Silently, she seethes.

She's perfect, and he's well up to the task
Of illustrating her full bloom of youth.
Why isn't she immortal then? you ask.
Look at her bedside table for the truth.

Carafe, decanter, bottle, beaker, all
Are brushed in with the same besotted touch:
Not just as clutter which, were it to fall,
Would break and be swept up. He cares too much

About the world around her. While she dreams,
The room dreams too, as if it too were spent
From pleasure. In the end, nothing redeems
This failure to make her the main event.

Manet's Olympia is no great shakes
For beauty beside this one, but transcends
Her setting with exactly what it takes:
The fire that starts where general interest ends.

Out for the count, Miss Italy sleeps on,
So lovely that we check the artist's name,
Vow to remember it, and then are gone,
Forgetting one who never found his fame

Because his unrestricted sympathy
Homogenised existence. Art must choose
What truly merits perpetuity
From everything that we are bound to lose.

Even a master's landscape, though devoid
Of people, has a human soul in view:
His own. A focussed vision is employed
To say: behold what I alone can do.

Picking the mortal to immortalise,
The great paint objects only to abet
Their concentration on what lives and dies.
Faced with a woman that they can't forget

They make sure we can't either. Should she rest,
Her daylight hours still dominate the room.
We see her waking up and getting dressed.
Her silence hits us like the crack of doom.

But this girl, drowned in decor, disappears
From memory, which doesn't care to keep
A pretty picture long, so save your tears.
I shouldn't try to wake her. Let her sleep,

And let Mancini, suave but second rate,
Sleep with her, as in fact he might have done –
Some recompense for his eventual fate
Of scarcely mattering to anyone.

Signed by the Artist

The way the bamboo leans out of the frame,
Some of its leaves cut short by the frame's edge,
Makes room for swathes of air which you would think,
If it were sold in bolts, would drape like silk.
Below, where one pond spills from the stone ledge
Into the next, three carp as white as milk
Glow through the water near the painter's name,
A stack of characters brushed in black ink.

The open spaces and the spare detail
Are both compressed into that signature:
He made his name part of the work of art.
Slice of crisp leaf, smooth flourish of fish fin
Are there to show you he is very sure
Of how the balance of things kept apart
Can shape a distance. On a larger scale
He still leaves out far more than he puts in.

We're lucky that he does. What he includes,
Almost too beautiful to contemplate,
Already hurts our hearts. Were he to fill
The gaps, the mind would have no place to rest,
No peace in the collected solitudes
Of those three fish, in how each leaf is blessed
With life. Easy to underestimate
A name like his. No substance. Too much skill.

The Australian Suicide Bomber's Heavenly Reward

Here I am, complaining as usual to Nicole Kidman
('Sometimes I think that to you I'm just a sex object')
While I watch Elle McPherson model her new range
Of minimalist lingerie.
Elle does it the way I told her,
Dancing slowly to theme music from *The Sirens*
As she puts the stuff on instead of taking it off.
Meanwhile, Naomi Watts is fluffing up the spare bed
For her re-run of that scene in *Mulholland Drive*
Where she gets it on with the brunette with the weird name.
In keeping with the requirements of ethnic origin
Naomi's partner here will be Portia de Rossi,
Who seems admirably hot for the whole idea.
On every level surface there are perfumed candles
And wind chimes tinkle on the moonlit terrace:
Kylie and Dannii are doing a great job.
(They fight a lot, but when I warn them they might miss
Their turn, they come to heel.)
Do you know, I was scared I might never make it?
All suited up in my dynamite new waistcoat,
I was listening to our spiritual leader –
Radiant his beard, elegant his uplifted finger –
As he enthrallingly outlined, not for the first time,
The blessings that awaited us upon the successful completion
Of our mission to obliterate the infidel.
He should never have said he was sorry
He wasn't going with us.
Somehow I found myself pushing the button early.
I remember his look of surprise
In the flash of light before everything went sideways,

And I thought I might have incurred Allah's displeasure.
But Allah, the Greatest, truly as great as they say –
Great in his glory, glorious in his greatness, you name it –
Was actually waiting for me at the front door of this place
With a few words of his own. 'You did the right thing.
Those were exactly the people to lower the boom on.
Did they really think that I, of all deities,
Was ever going to be saddled with all that shit?
I mean, *please*. Hello? Have we met?'
And so I was escorted by the Hockeyroos –
Who had kindly decided to dress for beach volleyball –
Into the antechamber where Cate Blanchett was waiting
In a white bias-cut evening gown and bare feet.
High maintenance, or what?
No wonder I was feeling a bit wrecked.
'You look,' she said, 'as if you could use a bath.'
She ran it for me, whisking the foam with her fingertips
While adding petals of hydrangeas and nasturtiums.
Down at her end, she opened a packet of Jaffas
And dropped them in, like blood into a cloud.

Windows Is Shutting Down

Windows is shutting down, and grammar are
On their last leg. So what am we to do?
A letter of complaint go just so far,
Proving the only one in step are you.

Better, perhaps, to simply let it goes.
A sentence have to be screwed pretty bad
Before they gets to where you doesnt knows
The meaning what it must of meant to had.

The meteor have hit. Extinction spread,
But evolution do not stop for that.
A mutant languages rise from the dead
And all them rules is suddenly old hat.

Too bad for we, us what has had so long
The best seat from the only game in town.
But there it am, and whom can say its wrong?
Those are the break. Windows is shutting down.

Anniversary Serenade

You are my alcohol and nicotine,
My silver flask and cigarette machine.
You watch and scratch my back, you scrub me clean.
I mumble but you still know what I mean.
Know what I mean?
You read my thoughts, you see what I have seen.

You are my egg-flip and my ego trip,
My passion-fruit soufflé and strawberry whip.
When the dawn comes to catch you on the hip
I taste the sweet light on my fingertip.
My fingertip?
I lift it to my quivering lips and sip.

Homecoming Queen and mother of our two
Smart daughters who, thank God, take after you,
This house depends on what you say and do –
And all you do is wise and say is true.
And say is true?
True as a plumb-line or a billiard cue.

On from Byzantium to Cooch Behar
Our Messerschmitt two-seater bubble car,
Laden with foie gras and with caviare,
Follows the shining road to Shangri-la.
To Shangri-la?
With Blossom Dearie singing in the bar.

When the sun fades, the Earth will fly away.
Tell me it isn't happening today.
I have a debt of happiness to pay.

I die if you should leave, live if you stay.
Live if you stay?
Live like a king, proud as a bird of prey.

My share of Heaven and my sheer delight,
My soda fountain and my water-sprite,
My curving ribbon of a climbing kite,
You are my Starlight Roof, my summer night.
My summer night?
The flying foxes glide, the possums fight.

You are my honeydew and panther sweat,
The music library on my private jet.
Top of the bill, we fly without a net.
You are the stroke of luck I can't forget.
I can't forget?
I'm still not ready for you even yet.

You are my nicotine and alcohol,
My Stéphane Audran in a Claude Chabrol,
My sunlight through a paper parasol,
My live-in living doll and gangster's moll –
And gangster's moll?
Mine the fedora, yours the folderol.

The ring is closed. The rolling dice we cast
So long ago still roll but not so fast.
The colours fade that we nailed to the mast
We lose the future but we own the past.
We own the past?
From our first kiss, a lifetime to the last.

Lock Me Away

In the NHS psychiatric test
For classifying the mentally ill
You have to spell 'world' backwards.
Since I heard this, I can't stop doing it.
The first time I tried pronouncing the results
I got a sudden flaring picture
Of Danny La Rue in short pants
With his mouth full of marshmallows.
He was giving his initial and surname
To a new schoolteacher.
Now every time I read the *Guardian*
I find its columns populated
By a thousand mumbling drag queens.
Why, though, do I never think
Of a French film composer
(Georges Delerue, pupil of
Darius Milhaud, composed the waltz
In *Hiroshima, Mon Amour*)
Identifying himself to a policeman
After being beaten up?
But can I truly say I never think of it
After I've just thought of it?
Maybe I'm going stun:
Dam, dab and dangerous to wonk.
You realise this ward you've led me into
Spelled backwards is the cloudy draw
Of the ghost-riders in the sky?
Listen to this palindrome
And tell me that it's not my ticket out.
Able was I ere I saw Elba.
Do you know who I am, Dr La Rue?

Sunday Morning Walk

Frost on the green.
The ducks cold-footing it across the grass
Beside the college moat

Meet a clutch of matrons
In freeze-dried Barbours
Walking their collies
Freshly brushed by Gainsborough.

Buoyed by the world's supply
Of rosemary sprigs
Packed under glass,

The moorcock emerging from the reeds
Does a hesitation step
As though dancing to Piazzolla.
Cool shoes, if I may say so.

In front of the boat-houses
The rowers rigging fulcrums to the shells
Bite off their gloves
To push in pins,

And the metal shines
Just short of a glitter
Because the light, though Croesus-rich,
Is kiss-soft.

Under the bridge, the iron ribs
Form a pigeon loft,
A pit-lane of sports saloons
Testing their engines.

The final year
Of the finishing school for swans
Passes in review,
Watched by the cob, his nibs,

Who at Bayreuth once
Had a glide-on role
In *Lohengrin*,
But this is better.

Winter regatta,
Unspoiled by even
Yesterday's litter
Spilling from the bins,

Is it any wonder
That I never left you?
Remember this day,
It's already melting.

Tramps and Bowlers

In the park in front of my place, every night
A bunch of tramps sleep on the wooden porch
Of the bowling green club-house. They shed no light.
No policeman ever wakes them with a torch,

Because no-one reports their nightly stay.
People like me who take an early walk
Just after dawn will see them start the day
By packing up. They barely even talk,

Loading their duffel bags. They leave no trace,
Thus proving some who sleep rough aren't so dumb.
Tramps blow their secret if they trash the place:
This lot make sure that, when the bowlers come,

There's not a beer-can to pollute the scene.
And so, by day, neat paragons of thrift
And duty bow down to the very green
Which forms, by night, for scruffs who merely drift,

Their front lawn. If the bowlers only knew,
For sure they'd put in for a higher fence.
They'd have a point, but it would spoil the view
More than the tramps will, if they have the sense

To keep on cleaning up before they go,
Protecting indolence with industry:
A touch of what the bowlers value so.
Which way of life is better? Don't ask me —

I chose both, so I'd be the last to know.

Portrait of Man Writing

While you paint me, I marvel at your skin.
The miracle of being twenty-four
Is there like a first blush as you touch in
The blemishes that make my face a war
I'm losing against time. So you begin,
By lending inwardness to an outline,
Your life in art as I am ending mine.

Try not to miss the story my mouth tells,
Even unmoving, of how once it had
The knack for spinning yarns and casting spells,
And had to make an effort to seem sad.
These eyes that look as crusty as dry wells
Despite the glue they seep, once keenly shone.
Give them at least a glimmer of what's gone.

I know these silent prayers fall on deaf ears:
You've got integrity like a disease.
Bound to record the damage of the years,
You aim to tell the truth, and not to please.
And so this other man slowly appears
Who is not me as I would wish to be,
But is the me that I try not to see.

Suppose while you paint me I wrote of you
With the same fidelity: people would say
That not a line could possibly be true.
Nobody's lips in real life glow that way.
Silk eyelashes! Is this what he's come to?
Your portrait, put in words, sounds like a lie,
Minus the facts a glance would verify.

But do we credit beauty even when
It's there in front of us? It stops the heart.
The mortal clockwork has to start again,
Ticking towards the day we fall apart,
Before we see now all we won't have then.
Let's break for lunch. What progress have we made?
Ah yes. That's me exactly, I'm afraid.

Mystery of the Silver Chair

As if God's glory, with just one sun-ray,
Could not burn craters in a chromosome,
We call it kindly when it works our way,
And, some of us with tact, some with display,
Arrange the house to make it feel at home.

With votive tokens we propitiate
Almighty God. Just to be neat and clean –
Running the water hot to rinse the plate,
Chipping the rust-flakes from the garden gate –
These things are silent prayers, meant to be seen.

Strange, though, when parents with a stricken child
Still cleanse the temple, purify themselves.
They were betrayed, but how do they run wild?
With Jay-cloth and a blob of Fairy Mild
They wipe the white gloss of the kitchen shelves.

They, least of all, are likely to let go
Completely, like the slovens down the street:
The ones who could conceal a buffalo
In their front lawn and you would never know,
Yet somehow they keep their Creator sweet.

Unjust, unjust: but only if He's there.
The girl with palsy looks you in the eye,
Seeming to say there is no God to care.
Her gleaming wheel-chair says He's everywhere,
Or why would the unwell try not to die?

And why would those who love them give the best
Years of their lives to doing the right thing?
Why go on passing a perpetual test
With no real hope and with so little rest?
Why make from suffering an offering?

Why dust the carpet, wash the car, dress well?
If God were mocked by those who might do that
With ample cause, having been given Hell
To live with, we could very quickly tell –
Somebody would forget to feed the cat.

Sometimes they do. Sometimes the spirit kneels.
But when those with the least take pride the most,
We need to bend our thoughts to how it feels.
Shamed by those scintillating silver wheels,
We see the lightning of the Holy Ghost.

The Genesis Wafers

Genesis carried wafers in her hold
To catch the particles sent from the sun.
Diamond, sapphire, gold
Were those fine webs, as if by spiders spun
Beside whom specks of dust would weigh a ton.

A million miles from Earth, in the deep cold,
The particles collected in the skeins.
Diamond, sapphire, gold,
They flowered like tiny salt pans in the rains –
Fresh tablecloths distressed with coffee stains.

Back in the lab, the altered wafers told
A story of how poetry is born:
Diamond, sapphire, gold
Serenities invaded by stuff torn
From the incandescent storm that powers the dawn.

Yusra

The Public Morals Unit of Hamas
Saw Yusra al-Azzuri, bold as brass,
In Gaza City, walk with her betrothed,
Her sister also present. Half unclothed,

All three behaved as if beyond the reach
Of justice. Laughing, dancing on the beach,
They almost touched. They thought to drive away.
The Unit followed them without delay.

Her young man drove. Beside him as they fled,
Yusra died quickly in a hail of lead.
The other two were hauled out of the car
And beaten senseless. With an iron bar,

The riddled corpse of Yusra, as the worst
Offender, was assaulted till it burst.
She would have prayed for death. It can be said,
Therefore, it was a blessing she was dead

Already. Thus we look for just one touch
Of grace in this catastrophe. Too much
To bear, the thought that those young men were glad
To be there. Won't the memory drive them mad?

Could they not see the laughter in her face
Was heaven on earth, the only holy place?
Perhaps they guessed, and acted from the fear
That Paradise is nowhere if not here.

Yusra, your name too lovely to forget
Shines like a sunrise joined to a sunset.
The day between went with you. Where you are,
That light around you is your life, Yusra.

The Nymph Calypso

Planning to leave Calypso in the lurch,
Odysseus snuck off to build a ship.
He found the right-shaped boughs of larch or birch
Or spruce, for all I know, from which to strip
The bark, and . . . but the details we can skip.
I won't pretend that I've done much research.
He had to build a ship and he knew how.
Just how he did it hardly matters now:

Enough to say he juggled rib and spar.
Calypso came to him and said, 'I see
That duty calls. Will you be going far?
You wouldn't have your mind on leaving me,
By any chance? Forget the trickery
For once, and if you're following your star
Just say so. Circe lured you with a song.
At least I wasn't stringing you along.'

'It's time,' he said. 'I'm an adventurer.
I sail in search of things. It's what I do.
I'd heard about how beautiful you were,
So lovely that I came in search of you.
But now I know you and need something new
To challenge me.' He wryly smiled at her
To show he knew he sounded like a ham.
'You wanted me. Well, this is what I am.'

'All very well,' Calypso said, 'but I
Have an investment here. You had to quit

Sometime, and I gave you a reason why.
Old studs like you need youth to love. I'm it.
I'm always eager, and you're still quite fit:
A last adventure to light up the sky.
I'll tell my tale forever, don't forget:
The greatest lover that I ever met.'

Odysseus could see the point, but still
He stood his ground, a man of destiny
Proclaiming his ungovernable will
To follow the unknown out to the sea
Beyond the sea, and solve the mystery
Of where the world went next, and not until
He had would he find rest. Calypso said,
'No wonder that you turned up here half dead.'

That night the two of them made love again.
She slapped herself against him when she came
The way she always did, but even then
She let him know she knew things weren't the same.
She cried out his polysyllabic name –
Something she'd never done for other men –
As if, this time, he was no longer there.
But though she flattered him with her despair,

Already he had made the break. His mind
Was elsewhere, on a course she could not guess.
She thought her hero had new worlds to find
Out on the edge of the blue wilderness,
But he had lied, to cause her less distress.
We needn't think of him as being kind:
He simply knew the truth would drive her mad
And make her fight with everything she had.

After he left, she let the world believe
She'd given him the boat: a likely tale
That Homer swallowed whole. Keen to deceive
Even herself, for no nymph likes to fail –
The Miss World of the Early Age of Sail
Had never yet known such a cause to grieve –
She spread the story that he'd only gone
Because she told him legends must go on.

But he was going home. There, in the end,
Lay the departure point for his last quest.
Age was a wound that time indeed would mend
But only one way, with a long, long rest.
For that, familiar territory is best.
As for Penelope, he could depend
On her care for the time he had to live.
Calypso wanted more than he could give,

And it was time to take, time to accept
The quiet bounty of domestic peace.
After he killed the suitors who had kept
His wife glued to the loom, she spread the fleece
Of their first blanket and they found release
Together as they once had. Though she wept
For their lost years, she gave him her embrace,
And he looked down into her ageing face

And saw Calypso. What the nymph would be,
Given the gift of time, was there made plain,
Yet still more beautiful. Penelope,
Because she knew that we grow old in pain
And learn to laugh or else we go insane,
Had life unknown to immortality,

Which never gets the point. 'Well, quite the boy,'
She murmured. 'And now tell me about Troy.'

Later the poets said he met his fate
In the Atlantic, or perhaps he went
Around the Horn and reached the Golden Gate.
Space vehicles named after him were sent
Into infinity. His testament,
However, and what truly made him great,
Was in the untold story of the day
He died, and, more or less, had this to say:

'Penelope, in case you ever hear
The nymph Calypso loved me, it was so:
And she tried everything to keep me near
But finally she had to let me go
Because she knew I loved you. Now you know,
And I can move on, having made that clear.'
And so he did, while she knelt by his side,
Not knowing, as he sailed on the last tide,

That just this once he almost hadn't lied.

As I See You

As I see you
Crystals grow
Leaves chime
Roses flow

As I touch you
Tables turn
Towers lean
Witches burn

As I leave you
Lenses shiver
Flags fall
Show's over